ST. ELIAS CHURCH
MUNHALL, PENNSYLVANIA

There are a number of HORIZON CARAVEL BOOKS published each year. Titles now available are:

American Heritage also publishes AMERICAN HERITAGE JUNIOR LIBRARY books, a similar series on American history. Titles now available are:

COVER: *The two-headed eagle was for nearly four centuries the symbol of czarist Russia.*

FRONT ENDPAPER: *The pomp and pageantry of the Russian Church are seen in this icon.*
A LA VIEILLE RUSSIE, NEW YORK

TITLE PAGE: *This drawing, from an old painting, shows a Kievan prince with his retinue.*
SOVFOTO

BACK ENDPAPER: *Czarist troops, and the winter, drove Napoleon's army out of Russia.*
MUSEE DE L'ARMEE, PARIS

A HORIZON CARAVEL BOOK

RUSSIA

UNDER THE CZARS

By the Editors of
HORIZON MAGAZINE

Author
HENRY MOSCOW

Consultant
CYRIL E. BLACK
Professor of History, Princeton University

ILLUSTRATED WITH MANY PAINTINGS,
PRINTS, ENGRAVINGS, AND MAPS OF THE TIMES

Published by American Heritage Publishing Co., Inc.
Book Trade and Institutional Distribution by
Harper & Row

FOURTH PRINTING
Library of Congress Catalog Card Number: 62–18602
© 1962 by American Heritage Publishing Co., Inc., 551 Fifth Avenue, New York, New
York 10017. All rights reserved under Berne and Pan-American Copyright Conventions.
Trademark CARAVEL registered United States Patent Office

FOREWORD

The aim of the Soviet Union today is to "overtake and surpass" the advanced countries of the West. Although that
slogan was invented by Communist leaders, it might well
have been proclaimed by the czars of Russia in earlier
centuries.

For much of their history the Russians have lived in
the shadow of more powerful neighbors. Therefore this
book begins with the story of a land in a defensive pos-
ture, of a people braced to resist the on-coming enemy.
It goes on to tell how in modern times the Russians have
waged another kind of war: they have strained their resources to the utmost to raise their standard of living,
to maintain and improve their international position, and
to spread their message abroad. This age-long effort to
contend with and surpass the West—despite the human
cost—has always been one of the main policies of Russian
leadership. Ivan IV in the sixteenth century was known
as the Terrible, and Peter I in the eighteenth century
as the Great, because of the ruthlessness and vigor of the
measures they took to strengthen the state and to battle
Russia's foreign enemies.

The story of Russia under the czars and under other
early rulers does indeed explain much of the Russians' behavior today. But the question of their future actions cannot
be answered. A knowledge of Russian history makes their
policies seem no more acceptable or their culture any more
like ours. We can, however, marvel at the fantastic con-
tradictions of Russia: the beauty that exists alongside the
cruelty, and the spirit of freedom that waits beneath the
generations of repression.

CYRIL E. BLACK

*Modern Russians, like these in Moscow's Red Square, are no longer ruled by
the czars; yet they are still dominated by the historic power of the state.*

This illumination from the menu used at Nicholas II's coronation banquet shows the royal couple and their courtiers all in ancient Russian costumes.

CONTENTS

I

ENEMIES OF THE CZARS

The two great armies stood ready, only a brief gallop apart, on a grassy plain north of the Black Sea in southern Russia. The decisive battle was at hand, and Darius the Great, riding at the head of the invaders, was impatient to begin.

Darius had good reason for his impatience. Master of thousands of fighting men, he had led about seventy thousand scimitar-armed cavalry and hard-muscled foot archers all the way from Persia to teach the strange Scythians who roamed the region not to overrun his country again and not to trade with his enemies the Greeks. But for many months of that year 512 B.C. he had been able to do nothing but chase the Scythians back and forth, hither and yon, while they pestered his troops but avoided pitched battle. Now at last he could finish the job for which he had come.

Suddenly a shout broke the silence in the Scythian ranks, then more shouts and whoops of glee. Scythian horsemen, clad in garments stitched from the scalps of slain foes, galloped about the plain, seemingly unmindful of Darius' troops. They were not attacking—they were chasing a hare. Darius shook his head. "These fellows hold us in deep contempt," he said sorrowfully. And his aide, Gobryas, responded that he had known all along the Scythians would be hard to deal with. The Scythians were indeed old hands at mocking their enemies.

A mysterious people who may have come from Darius' own Persia, these Scythians roved with their horses and cattle from China to the Danube as early as 800 B.C., hunting elk, bison, and bear, and fishing for sturgeon. In war each man drank the blood of the first enemy he killed and used the victim's skull as a wine cup. In peace the Scythians

This Russian bear was carved in the first century A.D. by an artist from the invading Sarmatian tribe.

Throughout history the Russians have fought bitterly to defend their home-land against invaders from both east and west. The deepest penetration of Russia from the west was made in 1812 by Napoleon's Grand Army (at left).

11

sheltered their wives and children in four- and six-wheeled wagons roofed with felt, carpeted with wool, and divided into compartments. Prosperous, they dressed their wives gaily and ordered intricately carved works of art from the goldsmiths of the Greek colonies on the shores of the Black Sea. They obeyed without question their leaders, who, like the later czars, ruled with cruel discipline; and they envied and suspected foreigners. In taste and in custom they resembled their descendants, the modern Russians. And in nothing is the resemblance stronger than in the military tactics the Scythians used on Darius, the Persian ruler.

When they first heard that Darius was coming, the Scythians had reasoned that, outnumbered, they would lose in pitched battle. So they had split their horsemen into three armies, under three kings, with orders to stay tantalizingly just out of Darius' reach. Whenever Darius had advanced toward one of the armies, the Scythians had retreated, burning the grass so his horses could find nothing to feed on and choking the wells and springs so his men could not drink from them.

The motherland of Russia is rich in relics from the warring peoples of her long and troubled past. Shown here are artifacts from the Scythian period. Below is a sword sheath that was used by a Scythian king. It has a battle scene carved into its gold surface. The circular plaque at left shows a Persian king chasing two wild boars. A carved bronze likeness of a gazelle being attacked by a lion is at the right.

In exasperation Darius had finally sent a challenge to one of the Scythian kings, Idanthyrsus: "Sir, these are strange doings. Why will you ever flee?"

The Scythian had sent back a scornful answer, recorded by the historian Herodotus:

"Know this of me, Persian, that I have never fled for fear of any man, nor do I now flee from you. But as to the reason why I do not straightway fight with you, this too I will tell to you. We Scythians have no towns or planted lands that we might meet you the sooner in battle, fearing lest the one be taken or the other be wasted. But if nothing will serve you but fighting straightway, we have the graves of our fathers. Come, find these and try to destroy them; then shall you know whether we will fight you for those graves or no. Till then we will not join battle unless we think good."

Almost immediately after that defiance, the Scythians stopped scorching the earth and retreating and turned to guerrilla warfare. The Persians had indeed reached into the Scythians' heartland, to the graves of their fathers—it was

time for the Scythians to gather their forces and fight.

Then the incident involving the hare took place. One Scythian army had moved to sabotage the Danube River boat bridge that Darius had built and without which he would have trouble returning home, even if he won. The two other Scythian armies had intensified their day and night raids on Darius' forces. To make sure that Darius did not withdraw before they wanted him to, they had left him tempting herds of cattle on which to feast. Then they had arrayed themselves for the great battle.

Whether the Scythians' pursuit of the hare was a trick or merely a demonstration of their self-confidence, it demoralized Darius. He never gave the order to attack. Instead, he withdrew silently in the night, ferrying his disordered troops across the Danube just ahead of the pursuing Scythians. The graves of the Scythians' fathers were safe. Darius never returned. And though some historians question Herodotus' details, it is clear that Darius had learned a lesson that many would-be conquerors have since had to relearn: people who rule and inhabit Russia, no matter what their racial origin, are hard to overcome. They defend their land as if it were in fact what they have long called it, Holy Mother Russia.

The love of the Russians for their country has more to do with its soil than with its government. And the soil seems never-ending: it sprawls over 8,600,000 square miles—making Russia the world's largest country (one sixth of the earth's land surface is Russian). But the soil is not generous. Only a relatively small part yields crops to feed Russia's 216,000,000 people, who are divided into no less than 108 distinct nationalities. Much of the soil lacks water, much of it is buried under snow eight months a year, and much of it is wasteland able to nourish only sparse grass waving weakly in the wind. Almost all of it lies north of our own chill Maine and North Dakota.

Furthermore, it is a soil that seems to welcome invaders, for it provides few natural defenses. In the extreme north lies the treeless, frozen tundra where only reindeer feel at home. In the south are mountains, forests, and deserts. The vast midland is steppe, or prairie, that stretches

The image of King Darius I is shown in relief on a column that once formed part of the Persian palace at Persepolis. Two attendants are behind Darius holding the imperial parasol. The royal palace was begun in 512 B.C., the year the Persians tried to conquer the Scythians in Russia. The structure was destroyed in 331 when Alexander the Great overran the Persian empire.

for thousands of miles. It is broken only by some broad rivers, by a few narrow belts of trees, and by the Ural Mountains, the average height of which is fifteen hundred feet (see map on page 30). The Urals, which run north and south to divide Europe from Asia, have never stopped anybody.

But the beckoning, easy-to-take look is deceptive. Defenders of Russian soil have a formidable ally in the climate. In the spring, melting ice and snow clothe the soil in slippery slush; in the autumn, rains turn the soil to waist-deep mud. Winter is worse. When Charles XII of Sweden was fighting Russia's Czar Peter the Great, birds froze as they flew, falling to earth dead. Charles' tough Swedes could not warm themselves outdoors because bonfires would not ignite, even in November. Like Darius, Charles eventually departed in disorderly flight. Few Russian winters are as bad as that of 1708–9 which Charles encountered, but Russia has the longest and coldest winters of any major country.

And the shrewd invader who attacks in June, as did Napoleon Bonaparte in 1812 and Adolf Hitler in 1941, must conquer quickly or not at all.

Napoleon, for one, harbored no doubts about quick conquest. The French emperor boasted to his marshals that he would "finish off, once and for all, the Colossus of Northern Barbarism." After conquering Russia he would be able to tackle England and eliminate the last great obstacle to his spreading empire. "In less than two months' time," he promised his doubting aide, General Armand de Caulaincourt, "Russia will be suing for peace." Only a few years before, he and Russia's Alexander I had met aboard a raft on the Niemen River, had embraced, and had sworn to be friends and allies forevermore. But the treaty they had signed was only a fragile piece of paper.

On the night of June 23, 1812, a few hours after he had made his boastful promise to de Caulaincourt, Napoleon sent the vanguard of his cavalry, artillery, and infantry rumbling over a pontoon bridge across the Niemen near Kovno, Lithuania, into Russian-held territory. On the Russian side a few scattered Cossacks—the only Russian troops in sight—did not deign to reply to the shots of Napoleon's forces.

Napoleon could hardly believe the scouts who brought word that the main Russian army had withdrawn, three days before, from Vilna, some sixty miles to the east. The invasion was going to be easier than he had expected.

Sweden's Charles XII was eighteen when he fought Peter the Great.

Across the vast midland belt where countless Russians fought off their enemy invaders, sheep graze peacefully on grass that grows thick and green in the fertile black soil.

Only five days later he had reason to think differently. Between Kovno and Vilna ten thousand of his horses perished, killed by exhaustion and cold night-rains. His once-vigorous young soldiers were collapsing and many were starving, for the supply wagons could not keep up with them. The heat that succeeded the cold rains made things even worse.

Napoleon pushed on, ever deeper into Russia. Occasionally the Russians paused to fight a rear-guard action. But, like the Scythians, they always withdrew. As important a city as Smolensk, halfway between Kovno and Moscow, and a holy place to Russians, was defended only

17

briefly and then abandoned in flames. Still Napoleon pushed on. Now the silent, deserted villages and market towns all were ablaze when he entered them, and Napoleon marveled at "a people who burn their houses to prevent our sleeping in them for a night."

It was September 7 before Napoleon could get the Russians to put up a real fight. Like Darius, he was eager for a decisive battle.

But that battle, fought at the village of Borodino, was fiercer than Napoleon had expected. For the Russians have always fought courageously when they thought that the time was right. De Caulaincourt, who was in the thick of the battle, wrote of the Russians: "Their ranks did not break; pounded by the artillery, sabred by the cavalry, forced back at the bayonet point by our infantry, their somewhat immobile masses met death bravely and only gave way slowly before the fury of our attacks."

Russian wounded disobeyed orders to quit the fight. One Russian officer had to use his sword on his own troops to make them retreat. Another officer raised an arm to point and a cannon ball carried it away; knocked from his horse, he pointed with his remaining arm.

When the battle ended and the Russians once again withdrew, the field was so thick with the dead that Napoleon's horse could scarcely find bare ground for its hoofs. Of their 111,000 men the Russians had lost 58,000—only 700 as prisoners. And of Napoleon's 130,000 soldiers he had lost 50,000, among them 49 generals dead or gravely wounded.

Remembering Borodino, Napoleon later said: "The most terrible of all my battles was the one before Moscow." But that was long afterward. Now, Moscow still lay ahead.

All along the road to Moscow, Russian peasants picked off laggard Frenchmen, often at the cost of their own lives. Guerrilla warfare had begun. And all along the road to Moscow, villages blazed; the thousands of Russian wounded who had sought shelter in the houses crawled away if they could, or died in the flames if they could not. The Russians still were scorching the earth.

At 10 A.M. on September 14, 1812, Napoleon was on the Sparrow Hills overlooking Moscow when a courier brought word that the Russian army had left the city. The

Brooding impatiently on a hilltop near Moscow, Napoleon awaits the return of his deputies with news that the city has surrendered. But to his dismay the Russians did not hand over Moscow; they left it deserted and in flames.

Russian commander, General Kutusov, had reasoned that "as long as the army exists and is in condition to oppose the enemy, we preserve the hope of winning the war; but if the army is destroyed, Moscow and Russia will perish."

Moscow would be in Napoleon's grasp without more trouble. Or so he thought. He sent an order into the city for officials and prominent citizens to meet him at the gate. No one came. He waited. Impatient, he dispatched officer after officer with similar orders. Still no Muscovites came. Except for a few ragged wretches it appeared that Moscow was deserted, a dead city, its eerie silence broken only by the hoofbeats of Napoleon's cavalry.

That night the Moscow bazaar burned. Then two small blazes started in the suburbs. The men were cautioned to be more careful with their campfires. The next day Napoleon moved into the czars' apartments in the Kremlin. That night too, about eight o'clock, a fire started in a suburb. But the weary Napoleon and his officers went to bed early, merely annoyed at what they thought was their troops' carelessness. De Caulaincourt's valet awakened him at ten thirty. The city was burning. Then, as a furious, shifting wind spread the flames, French soldiers began

bringing in Russian policemen and peasants under arrest. They had been caught setting fires.

Looking out a window of the Kremlin, which itself was partly ablaze, Napoleon saw columns of smoke obscuring the glow the flames cast on the citadel's golden domes. "What a people!" he commented, according to the Russian historian Eugene Tarle. "They are Scythians!"

In the one sixth of Moscow that remained standing amid the charred ruins, Napoleon waited. Surely now Alexander I would be willing to make peace, and Napoleon sent emissaries to the capital at St. Petersburg suggesting a friendly settlement. Outside Moscow some of the Cossack cavalry were fraternizing with the French, and the weather, though winter should have come, remained so warm that Napoleon talked of staying in Moscow until spring.

Suddenly, disaster struck. Instead of replying to Napoleon's peace offers, the Russians swooped down in a surprise attack on the army of Napoleon's General Murat outside Moscow and defeated him ignominiously.

Napoleon was shaken. He had been expecting peace, and now he was facing a prolonged war. He was far from his bases of supply, and devastated Russia would not feed

STATE HISTORICAL MUSEUM, MOSCOW

Napoleon found so much of Moscow in ruins that he had to stable his horses in the Ouspensky Cathedral (left). When he quit the city in October, 1812, his soldiers had to sleep in the snow as well as march in it (above). Many froze to death; others starved when blizzards wrecked supply lines.

Russian patriots fight French soldiers inside the Kremlin, while all around them Moscow burns. The fire was

pread by winds that changed direction three times in one night. Nearly all of the buildings were leveled.

his army. The news from Spain, where his armies were fighting on another front, was bad. Like Darius, he made a sudden decision. On the night of October 19 Napoleon's Grand Army began to retreat from Moscow—100,000 troops followed by a huge baggage train filled with loot.

The fine weather changed to snow. The temperature dropped as low as 40 degrees below zero. The horses had no fodder and the men grew so hungry in the ruined countryside that they carved the flesh from fallen animals. For shelter they sometimes built huts of frozen corpses stacked like logs. Wagons crashed through the ice on the rivers,

The French retreat from Moscow is the subject of this famous work by the painter Meissonier. Grim-faced as he sits astride his white charger, Napoleon leads the remnants of his Grand Army across the muddy Russian landscape to safety beyond the Berezina River.

and the survivors envied those who had perished. Wounded men were picked up and loaded onto wagons so crowded that there was room only on the outside. And when they jolted off, the wagons did not stop; the wounded were left in the road to be trampled by the remainder of the procession. And always the retreat was harried by Russian troops and by furious peasants, even by women swinging scythes to mow down the tormented, beaten invaders.

Napoleon himself, accompanied by de Caulaincourt, arrived at the Tuileries Palace back in Paris just before midnight on December 18, 1812. Personally, Napoleon and de Caulaincourt had suffered only a small part of the agony of the troops, but they were so changed that the palace porter who opened the door, lamp in hand, had to call his wife to help identify them.

Of Napoleon's Grand Army—the 420,000 men who had started across the Niemen in June and the 150,000 who had reinforced them later—only 30,000 fighting men were left.

It is often said that the only thing we learn from history is that we do not learn from history; the saying applies to those enemies of the czars who have sought to conquer Russia. Napoleon knew about Darius and he knew about Charles XII. Adolf Hitler knew about Napoleon and presumably about Darius and Charles. But on June 22, 1941, Hitler sent the troops of Nazi Germany, to the rumble of tanks and artillery, marching into Russia.

At first it seemed that Hitler's invasion would succeed. In a few weeks whole Russian armies had been surrounded, tens of thousands of prisoners taken, airfields and bridges captured. By October, German tanks—roaring over the very roads that Napoleon's cavalry had ridden—were only forty miles from Moscow. All Russia would surely fall before winter.

Then the Russian rains began. The Nazis' tanks stuck in the mud. The rain turned to snow and ice. Through their obscured peepholes the German tank drivers could make out the golden, onion-shaped domes of Moscow. But they never got closer than the city's suburbs, for suddenly a hundred fresh Russian divisions sent them reeling back.

To the south, where it was warmer, the Germans pushed through the heavy rains into Rostov, at the mouth of the Don River. Then another sudden Russian attack drove them out in a fifty-mile retreat.

Behind the German lines, Russian guerrillas compounded the misery that cold, snow, and hunger were in-

flicting on the invaders. Garbed as peasants, as beggars, even as Nazi stormtroopers, they annihilated German detachments in swift raids or cut supply and communication lines. Hitler now knew it would not be so easy.

But if he could capture the oil-rich Caucasus in southern Russia, he could win. The key to the Caucasus was the city of Stalingrad (which the Russians, in belated disavowal of their late dictator Joseph Stalin, renamed Volgograd in 1961). Hitler's Sixth Army attacked Stalingrad in September, 1942. Artillery and airplanes shelled and bombed the city's buildings into rubble, and the Nazi infantry moved in. But the Russians fought them hand to hand in the ruins. For weeks, for months, one of history's greatest battles raged. Then Russian reinforcements from north and south closed in on Hitler's troops. The Germans tried a counterattack to roll back the forces that surrounded them. They failed.

A few thousand German wounded were airlifted out of the besieged city. But then fog grounded the planes, and the Russians seized the airfields. Escape from Stalingrad was now impossible. And as the Germans weakened from the

hunger and the cold they realized that surrender was the only choice open to them. On February 2, 1943, the fighting finally ceased, and 91,000 men gave themselves up to the Russians.

Meanwhile, the rest of Hitler's forces in Russia, along with the German army that had tried to relieve Stalingrad, were retreating on a wide front. Their march was as horror-filled and as chaotic as Napoleon's withdrawal from Moscow. In mud-stained, bloody shreds of uniforms the defeated Germans staggered westward, back into Europe.

Stalingrad cost Hitler 330,000 men, and it was, says Heinz Schröter, a German correspondent who was there, "the battle that changed the world." For Adolf Hitler it was the beginning of the end.

Napoleon laid his defeat in Russia to the winter weather; it is said that after Stalingrad Hitler could not bear to look at snow. Neither conceded enough credit to the doggedness of Russians defending the graves of their fathers. Both of these foreign enemies made the mistake of forgetting that the Russians have accepted many hardships under the czars and throughout their history—but they have always been "hard to deal with" for their conquerors.

Hitler's attempt to conquer Russia was no more successful than former invasions had been. The Russian weather crippled the Nazi onslaught. When winter snows had melted, the German army found itself wallowing in mud that disabled weapons and paralyzed tanks (left). Russia's climate and geography have always helped her repel invaders, but the key to her invincibility has been the will of her people to resist. At Stalingrad (below) they fought fiercely until the Nazi army was finally beaten.

ПЛѢНЪ РѸСКЫ

НАЖЬ ВЪ ДРЪСТРѢ

II

THE HOUSE OF RURIK

Among the first men to live on Russian soil were the Slavs. These fair-haired people of obscure origin began spreading over the steppes and through the northern forests from the river basins northeast of the Carpathian Mountains in the first century A.D. They preferred farming to fighting, but there were many strange and savage tribes, as ferocious as the Slavs were peaceable, who contested their fields. Sharp, primitive battles ensued, followed by periods of peace in which the Slav strain was intermixed with the blood of others. The Russians who endured life under the czars—and the Russians of today—were the result.

Herodotus records the earliest blending of the various Russian forebears. The Scythians, he says, discovered one day that the armored soldiers of the invading Sarmatians from Persia were girls. Unwilling to fight women, they sent one of their handsomest young men to await an enemy scout. When one rode up, the Scythian youth indicated by signs that he was unarmed and wanted to be friendly. And when they parted, the Sarmatian girl indicated that if the Scythian would return tomorrow with a friend, she would bring one too. Thus gradually the Scythians and the Sarmatians became a single people, and one of their nomadic tribes, the tall, blond Alans, dominated the southern steppes until the savage Goths from what is now Germany descended on them in the third century. Like Scythians and Sarmatians, Goths and Alans became allies, only to give way before the Huns, a hideous, big-headed, bow-legged tribe from Central Asia who slept on horseback and never

Europeans look east (arrow) into Russia's vast land that extends 5,300 miles to the tip of Asia and covers one sixth of the globe.

OVERLEAF: *The Goths stormed into Russia from Germany's Baltic Sea coast (bottom); other tribes marched, rode, or sailed in across the open frontiers to harry and to merge with the Slavs. On this map the major battles of Russian history are marked by crossed swords.*

Riding out with his helmeted knights, Svyatoslav is shown on a white horse in the manuscript painting at left (top). He brought peace to the early Russian state of Kiev by overcoming fierce tribes like the Bulgars (bottom).

Siberia

Ural Mts.

Kazan

N. Dvina

Archangel

Ocean Trade Route

Moscow

St. Petersburg

Smolensk
1812

Novgorod

Pskov

Finland

Russia

Varangians

Baltic Sea

Sweden

Russia's History
IN GLOBAL PERSPECTIVE

Norway

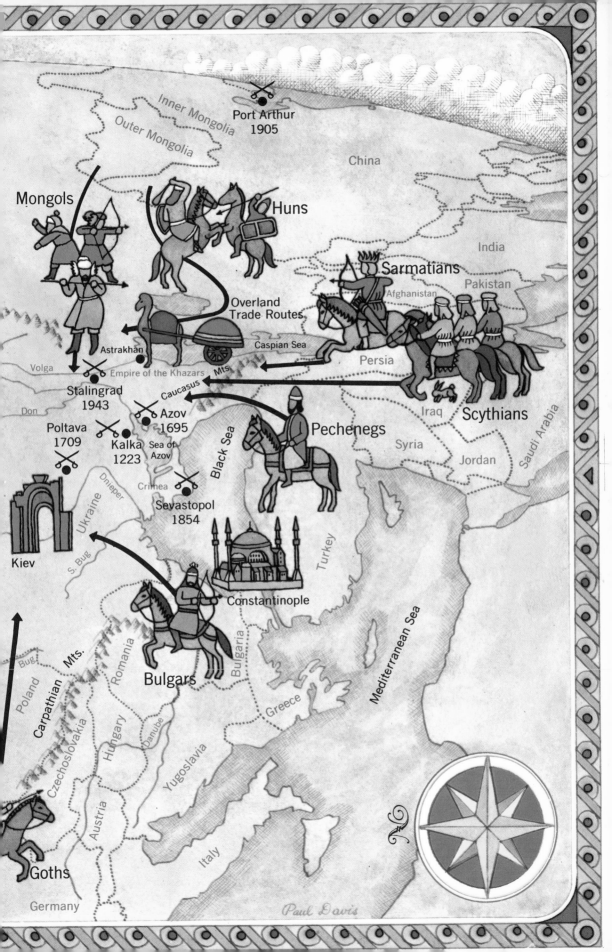

Ukraine in Pictures, BORETSKY, 1954

The Golden Gate of Kiev, built in 1037, still stands as a symbol of Russian freedom before the czars. Here the Slavs found a safe refuge.

changed their clothes. The Huns in turn gave way before the Bulgars, a people much like themselves, with whom they partly merged.

An even more ferocious folk, the Avars, who harnessed captive women to chariots, next surged out of the Mongolian deserts onto the steppes, extending their mastery as far west as the Baltic Sea. Toward the end of the sixth century, even the proud emperors of Byzantium, ruling from Constantinople, felt it wise to yield to the Avars' arrogant demand for 120,000 gold pieces a year, along with an elephant and a bed of solid gold for their king. Then their glory too passed: as a tribe they vanished so completely that modern Russians use the Avars' name instead of the dodos' to indicate that something is thoroughly dead. But some Avar blood, like that of the Scythians, the Sarmatians, the Huns, the Bulgars, and dozens of other tribes that swept onto the Russian grasslands with their herds, runs today in the veins of modern Slavs, the most numerous people in Europe.

Out of the centuries-long fury of rearing horses and savage cries, of flashing swords and falling heads, emerged Russia's first civilization, that of the Khazars. A conglomeration of remnants of Huns, Bulgars, and Turks, the Khazars moved in on the heels of the Avars, and in the seventh century began settling on the shores of the Black, Caspian, and Azov seas and in the region between the Don and Volga rivers. Belying their murderous, nomadic ancestry, they ruled the Slavs with a mild hand. On the lower Volga they built their capital city, Itil, from which they exported furs, hides, fish, honey, wax, and slaves downriver to Constantinople in exchange for fine wines, spices, brocaded silks, and jewels. They won a reputation for treating all men fairly. When the Christian Emperor Leo III expelled the Jews from Constantinople in 721, the Khazars welcomed the refugees. Later, after hearing the arguments of Christian, Moslem, and Jewish sages, the Khazar king and his court adopted Judaism. But they allowed all citizens to follow whatever faith they preferred. The Khazars grew so important that Emperor Constantine V of Byzantium married a Khazar princess, and their son became Byzantium's Emperor Leo IV (775–780). And so broad was the Khazar domain that it extended all the way to the Slav town of Kiev, far to the west, on the right bank of the Dnieper River in the fertile region of southwestern Russia that is now called the Ukraine, a name which means "borderland." From the disintegration of Khazaria, Kiev was to survive, to become one of the foundation stones of modern Russia.

When Kiev began, nobody knows, but Roman coins from the third century have been dug from its soil. It might have remained an inconsequential place but for a single, virtually forgotten battle. After eighty years of warring on the Khazars, the Arab torchbearers of Mohammed's new religion, Islam, won a major battle against them in 737, taking prisoner and enslaving twenty thousand Slav soldiers of the Khazar army. Many of the escaping Slavs doubtless fled toward Kiev, seeking more dependable protectors than the Khazars. They found them in the Norsemen, or Scandinavian Vikings, who had been roving the great river highways of Russia for several hundred years, trading, marauding, or serving as armed guards for the voyage to Constantinople. By the middle of the ninth century they had established themselves in the Slav towns

The early Russians searched for new gods and leaders. The Khazarians turned to Judaism; the bold Norsemen (above) worshiped idols.

THE GLORY OF THE CHURCH

Throughout the centuries of the rule of the czars in Russia, and ever since Vladimir brought the Eastern branch of Christianity to Kiev from Constantinople in the tenth century, the Russians have been captivated by the beauty and power of the Church. Vladimir's son, Yaroslav the Wise, commissioned architects to design the Church of St. Sophia in Kiev (above and left) in the style of St. Sophia in Constantinople (right). Later czars used the authority of the Church to bolster their rule.

along the river road from Novgorod to Kiev, and even as far south as the Black Sea.

Then, according to the ancient Russian Chronicle, around 859 the Slavs of Novgorod revolted against the Vikings who were in the service of the city and drove them out. The result was chaos. After the revolt, the Chronicle records: "There was no law among them . . . and they began to war against one another. They said to themselves, 'Let us seek a prince who may rule over us according to the law.' They went overseas to the Varangian Russes and said, 'Our land is great and rich, but there is no order in it. Come to rule and reign over us.' "

By "our land" they meant most of the region that came to be known as Kievan Rus (see map on page 40). They called the Norsemen Varangians from the Norse word *vaeringjar*, which means "sworn men"—a band of a hundred or so who swore obedience to a leader. Why they called them Russes is debatable. Some historians trace the word Rus to the Finnish *ruotsi*, for "rowers"; others say it derives from *Ros*, or *Rokhs*, the name of an Alan clan. In any case, the Chronicle says that "our land" was so troubled that the Norse adventurers who were invited to rule Novgorod agreed only with reluctance. Rurik, the Norse chieftain, stayed in Novgorod and became its prince. The House of Rurik was to reign over Russia until 1598, its Norse origin completely submerged by Russianism.

Rurik died in 879, and his kinsman Oleg—taking power until Rurik's infant son, Igor, could grow up—sailed down the river to Kiev. He lured Askold and Dir, two Swedes who ruled the town, onto his boat, killed them, and made himself Kiev's grand prince. But like the grand princes who came after him, he did not sit on a throne in regal robes, administering justice and distributing largess. These forerunners of the czars, Kiev's early Norse princes, straddled horses, in warrior garb, and waved lances instead of scepters. With their bodyguards of freebooting boyars, or knights, they exacted rich tribute as they traveled from settlement to settlement, amassing goods to ship to Constantinople.

Igor, in fact, was slain when he tried to collect twice in one short period from the same settlement. But his son Svyatoslav continued in his family's rugged tradition. "Upon his expeditions he carried with him neither wagons nor kettles and boiled no meat, but cut off small strips of horseflesh, game, or beef and ate it after roasting it on the coals. Nor did he have a tent, but he spread out a horse-

Slavs heaped treasure at the feet of Rurik, according to legend, and begged him to rule over them. The fact may be that Rurik's Vikings became the Slavs' rulers by force.

Rurik's grandson Svyatoslav (bare-headed, above) commanded a warrior band of both Slavs and Norsemen. Their equipment was mixed and informal: most had lances, helmets, and shields; some even had mail shirts and shortswords.

Civilization came to uncultivated Kiev from Constantinople. Below, a Kievan princess is shown being converted to Christianity amid Byzantine riches. At right is a bejeweled, fur-trimmed hat alleged to have belonged to the last great ruler of Kiev, Vladimir Monomakh.

blanket under him and set his saddle under his head," one of the ancient Chronicles records.

Though Constantinople was a good customer, the grand princes repeatedly attacked her—and on at least one occasion fled in terror when the city's defenders sprayed them with "Greek fire," a forerunner of napalm and the flame thrower. Svyatoslav also sacked the Khazar capital of Itil, which was still a rival for the Constantinople trade. And twice he invaded Bulgaria, the land where the fierce Bulgars had settled. Constantinople was able to control the Kievan princes by treaty and by granting them certain privileges when they came to trade.

Svyatoslav, like his father, died in the saddle. Bound home to Kiev in 972, after having been expelled from Bulgaria, he was ambushed by Pechenegs, another savage nomadic tribe that roved the steppes. In Scythian fashion, a Pecheneg prince made a gilded drinking cup of Svyatoslav's skull.

It was under the leadership of Rurik's great-grandson Vladimir that Kiev emerged into civilization. Vladimir was a lusty fellow who acquired several official and eight hundred unofficial wives, often by force. He hunted, feasted, and slaughtered Christians, all with equal zest. Then, under the influence of Byzantium, he adopted Christianity and had himself and his people, whether they liked it or not, baptized in the Greek Orthodox faith. He imported priests and made education—the first education that Russia had known—compulsory for the sons of priests and boyars. Churches rose, and Vladimir taxed the people to support them. When a German bishop visited Kiev shortly before Vladimir's death, he reported that the city boasted four hundred churches and eight markets. Another tourist, Adam of Bremen, likened Kiev to "that shining glory of the East, Constantinople." Most important of all, two Greek Orthodox missionary brothers, Cyril and Methodius, devised an alphabet, the Cyrillic, which gave the Slavs their first written language and permitted them to read the Scriptures without learning Greek.

Vladimir's son, Yaroslav the Wise (1019–54), continued the civilizing of Kievan Rus. Under Church influence, he initiated a legal code to replace the barbaric practices still in fashion. The code, *Russkaia Pravda* ("Russian Justice"), set fixed punishments for offenses, provided no death penalty, and even gave women certain rights— though the killing of a woman remained a lesser crime than the killing of a man. Yaroslav built more churches, a

The states of Kievan Rus (gray area) occupied only a small part of modern Russia. They·extended north and south from Novgorod to Kiev and eastward beyond Moscow.

In Novgorod a bell called men to the veche, a kind of town meeting.

library, and a divinity school. He tightened his control over the scattered cities and settlements that looked to Kiev as their capital, and he gave Kievan Rus the semblance of a national state. More, he gave it the semblance of a world power by taking a Swedish princess for a bride and by marrying his sister to the king of Poland and his three daughters to the kings of France, Norway, and Hungary. Controlling the booming waterway traffic to the south, Kiev was becoming larger than London or Paris.

For ordinary men, who before the days of Vladimir had lived little better than hunted beasts of the steppe and forest, life became good. In the countryside free peasants farmed their own lands, and prisoners of war and bankrupts and offenders against law who tilled the boyars' estates as slaves could become free. In the cities and towns artisans prospered. No man's place in society was fixed by his birth. The industrious craftsman could become a well-off member of the middle class, the shrewd peasant a landowner or even a boyar.

A primitive democracy began taking shape in the institution called the *veche*, which resembled a New England town meeting, in purpose if not in decorum. In all the cities of Kievan Rus, the *veche*—comprised of adult, free males— gathered in the main square at the clang of a bell to vote on civic affairs. The *veches* became so important later on that they sometimes rejected princes and dictated contract terms to those whom they accepted. Kievan Rus was almost a land of liberty.

But Yaroslav the Wise had made one grave mistake. Before he died in 1054, he wanted to avoid the fraternal quarrels over the throne which had always beset the House of Rurik. So he divided his domain among his five sons; thus each ruled only a fraction of Kievan Rus. And whether it was Yaroslav's doing or not, a new system of succession apparently came into force about this time: a prince's brothers, rather than his sons, inherited his authority. The eldest surviving brother got the biggest princedom, the next eldest the next biggest, and so on. When one died, the brothers below him in seniority all moved up a peg, changing thrones. The intent was good: it was to prevent any

This is the earliest combat scene pictured in Russian art. Done by an unknown artist, it shows a battle of 1169 between two of Kiev's dependencies, Novgorod and Suzdal. At top, the citizens of Novgorod parade their holiest icon, or religious painting. In the center, negotiations between the two sides are broken off as the soldiers of Suzdal shoot arrows at the icon. At bottom, the soldiers of Novgorod attack, assisted by an angel hovering above.

one prince from making all the land his immediate family's private preserve. But families were huge, jealousies strong. Middle-aged sons resented youthful uncles who outranked them and would probably outlive them, forever keeping them from a throne. They fought one another, often in alliance with foreign princes, and enslaved one another's followers and peasants. They had to fight constantly against the Cumans, or Polovtsy, a savage nomad people of the steppes who despoiled towns and villages and carried off their populations. Once again living in fear and dread, as they had before Vladimir's conversion to Christianity, people began to flee the land. Kievan Rus was declining.

New cities, rising to the north, northeast, and northwest, were virtually independent of Kiev. One prince of the House of Rurik, who ruled a newly founded town called Vladimir, even led an expedition against Kiev in 1169,

In 1043, when Kievan power was at its peak, Prince Vladimir aided a group of Byzantine rebels against their emperor. In the upper part of this miniature the emperor's army is setting out to fight the Kievans. Below, after Vladimir's victory, the two sides meet to negotiate a peace.

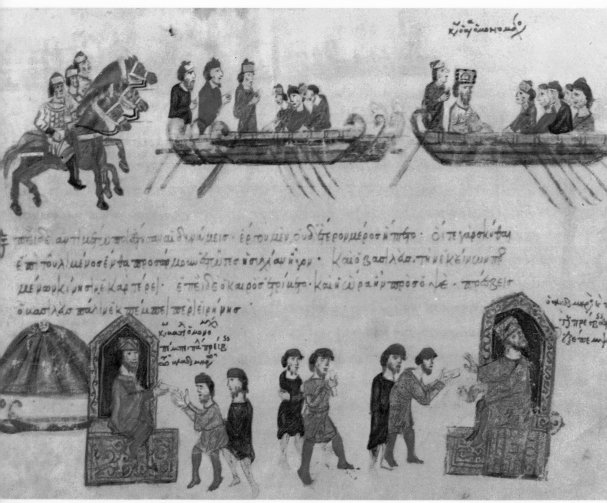

massacred hundreds of Kievans, and pillaged the city's remaining wealth. When the Western Christians of the Fourth Crusade ravaged and robbed Constantinople in 1204, Kiev's trade with Constantinople—the very basis of its livelihood—disappeared. Emigration accelerated, while new invaders, this time from the north and west, began pushing into what remained of Kievan Rus.

And far, far away to the east, in the Gobi Desert on the border of China, a young boy, constantly in flight from the slayers of his chieftain father, was growing up precariously. His ambitions eventually would change the history not only of Kiev but of all Russia, and would add still another Oriental strain to the blood of the Russian people and their rulers, still new strengths and weaknesses to the young Russian nation. His name was Temujin and he was to become Genghis Khan, "the Power of God on Earth."

As Kiev declined, the princes of the House of Rurik began to fight with one another rather than against foreign enemies. At left is a fierce clash of arms outside the gate of Kiev.

III   IVAN THE TERRIBLE

The Mongol ruler Genghis Khan hoped to bring first Russia, then all of the known world, into his empire.

When Genghis Khan was born in 1162, Paris was starting to build the Cathedral of Notre Dame. Venice was a rich merchant republic. Spain was fighting to liberate herself from Moorish invaders. England, under King Henry II, was transforming feudal anarchy into national order.

But in Mongolia, Genghis Khan's birthplace far to the east of Kievan Rus, men lived like Scythians, sheltering their women and children in tents and driving their herds over sparse plains. And Moscow, on the edge of Russia's northwestern forests, was a raw, tiny settlement behind wooden palisades on the hill where the Kremlin now stands.

The dreams of Genghis Khan and the destiny of Moscow were intermingled, although Genghis Khan was long dead when his descendants came to dominate Moscow.

Brave, intelligent, persuasive, and hardened by his youthful years of struggle to stay alive, Genghis Khan welded scattered Mongol tribes into a single fighting force and conquered much of civilized China. Then, enlisting China's skills and manpower, he set out to impose a Mongol peace on the world. He almost succeeded. Before he died, his empire sprawled from Korea to the Dnieper River and down into India, and under his heirs it took in lands as distant as Tibet, Mesopotamia, and Poland.

The Mongols first thundered into Russia in 1223, while Genghis Khan still lived, and quickly showed what kind of people they were. Defeating a Russian force in a three-day battle at the river Kalka, they captured three Russian princes. Their custom forbade them to shed the blood of rulers, so they laughingly used the three princes as foundations for a platform on which the Mongols feasted to celebrate their victory. The princes were crushed to death, their blood unshed.

The Mongols came again in 1237, burning, killing, enslaving. Militarily they were magnificent. Prideful, disciplined, their cavalry maneuvered with the precision of a ballet, advancing and withdrawing to make their victims

After many defeats, the Russians (above at left) scored a victory in 1380 over their invaders from the East.

expose unprotected flanks. They yielded few prisoners; if one man in a squad of ten let himself be captured, the other nine were executed. Attacking a fortified place, they built a wall around it to protect their men and to prevent the enemy's escape. For four years they laid waste town after town, city after city.

The Russians fought them with the contemptuous spirit of the Scythians. When the Mongols demanded that the little principality of Ryazan surrender 10 per cent of its wealth, the princes answered: "When there are none of us left, then all will be yours."

No Russians resisted harder than the Kievans. Working in day-and-night shifts, the Mongols belabored the city's stockade with battering rams. When the stockade finally fell, the Kievans fought from behind a second, inner wall built during the battle. The Mongols beat down the second wall. The Kievans fled to the churches. Men, women, and children were slaughtered before the altars. Only two hundred houses remained standing in Kiev, and years afterward, whitened skulls and bones littered the deserted city.

The Mongols did not come to settle. They sought slaves, soldiers, and tribute. As for ruling, they were content

The Mongols were depicted variously by artists in the many countries they overwhelmed. The warriors at left are from a thirteenth-century Japanese scroll. The Mongol camp above is from a twelfth-century Chinese painting.

The Kievans fought desperately to defend their city, but they were forced to succumb to the Mongols' superior strength and weapons. The invaders conquered the city, torturing and killing its inhabitants.

to do that through Russian princes, and they found princes willing to collaborate because there seemed no other possible course.

The case of Alexander Nevsky is an example. When the Mongols were advancing in 1237, the Swedes thought the time ripe to sail against Novgorod. Alexander, Prince of Novgorod, was little more than a boy. But in July, 1240, he sank some of the Swedes' ships on the Neva River—and drove off the rest. From that time on he was known as Alexander Nevsky (or of the Neva).

After the Swedes, German knights from the Baltic attacked. Nevsky sent the Germans fleeing across the ice of Lake Peipus. Next came Lithuanians. Nevsky, with an army scarcely bigger than a bodyguard, beat them too.

But even Alexander Nevsky knew it would be senseless to take on the Mongols. When, impressed by his valor and wisdom, the Mongols named him Grand Prince of Vladimir, he accepted willingly. He went further: in 1257 the Mongols sent envoys to Novgorod to demand tribute, and the people rioted, threatening to kill the emissaries. By persuasion and force Alexander pacified them, and over the years he performed the same service again and again for his Eastern masters. But when he died in 1263, a great Russian churchman declared, "The sun of Russia has set." And who is to say whether Alexander was traitor or savior, a knave or a wise man who made the best of bad days?

Despite Genghis Khan's dream of a Mongol peace, the two and one-half centuries of the "Mongol yoke" brought little peace to Russia. Russian princes fought among themselves, often seeking Mongol support against their own countrymen. Rivalries troubled the Mongols too. Regional khans, though they owed allegiance to the same great khan, fought each other with Russian help. The Mongols continued to feast, figuratively, on a platform built over living Russian bodies. But the feasters grew leaner and leaner, while the men beneath grew stronger and stronger.

After more than a hundred years of occupation, the Mongols finally abandoned western Russia, including Kiev, Smolensk, and the major water routes. The Lithuanians and the Poles, who succeeded the Mongols in power, indelibly marked the western Russians with their own culture and way of life. Moscow, located in central Russia, though still under loose Mongol control, went pretty much its own way. But in the southeast, near the site of Stalingrad, the Mongols held on under the name of the Golden Horde. The Golden Horde itself, however, had broken away from the great khan, and its forces now were largely Turks and Tatars, so the Russians began to speak of their masters as Tatars.

The central Russians toppled the platform in 1480, though the khans continued to plague parts of Russia as late as the nineteenth century. But the Russia that freed itself was vastly changed from the days of Kiev's glory. Demands for slaves and soldiers had drained the country's manpower. The steppes were deserted, for people had fled to the cities close to the northern forests, and many of the cities themselves were in ruins.

The flight to the cities had helped Moscow to grow, just as Kiev had grown when Slav refugees had gone there from Khazaria for protection four centuries earlier. In fact, much of Moscow's population had come from Kiev.

Moscow was an unlikely candidate for greatness. It was far inland and it sat on an unimportant river, the Moskva. It had therefore never known the mercantile wealth of Novgorod; neither had it developed the culture of Kiev.

Alexander Nevsky (with his family above) pacified the angry Eastern hordes so Russia could enjoy a period of peace.

Ivan IV (above), known as the Terrible, had the power to destroy his enemies—and he almost destroyed Russia too.

Moscow possessed a great asset, however, in the purposefulness of its princes, who had had their eyes on power all the while that they had submitted to their Mongol overlords. Even more important was the lesson Moscow had learned from Mongol rule: the need for national unity. Thus, when another of Rurik's strong-willed descendants, Ivan III, came to the throne in 1462, he was determined to give national unity to all of Russia.

Ivan is now remembered as Ivan the Great. The principality over which he ruled was called Muscovy, whose capital was Moscow. He immediately set about seizing city after city, region after region, from fellow princes—and local opinion was usually behind him. Novgorod, proud and with an independent spirit, was the only city that held out for a long time. But, needing the food supplies that Ivan's Muscovy controlled, even Novgorod eventually submitted.

By overcoming rival princes, by warring on Lithuania and Poland to regain Russian lands in the west, Ivan tripled Muscovy's domain during his forty-three-year reign. By marrying the pope's ward, who was also the niece of Byzantium's last emperor, he enhanced his own and the country's prestige. And by importing Greek and Italian architects to build churches and palaces he transformed Moscow into a place of some splendor, despite its hovels and its mud.

Yet Ivan unintentionally built into the new Russian nation a dangerous weakness. Though he had been crowned as Grand Prince, he began calling himself Czar, a corruption of the word Caesar. He reduced his rival princes, who had equal claim to descent from Rurik, to the status of boyars. These great landowners made up the country's hereditary ruling class; Ivan's downgrading of their rank would later bring much grief to Russia. Ivan's first act upon asserting his dominion over Novgorod was to jail its woman mayor and to move to Moscow the bell that had summoned Novgorod's city assembly. "There shall be no *veche* and no bell in our land of Novgorod," he proclaimed. No longer could all Novgorod's males meet in the central square to vote on the city's problems.

Ivan thus swung Russia away from democracy toward dictatorship and autocracy. But it remained for Ivan's grandson, known as Ivan the Terrible, to try to make the power of the czar absolute. The British historian Lord Acton said, "Power tends to corrupt; absolute power corrupts absolutely." He may well have had in mind Ivan IV,

Construction of the Kremlin (below), a citadel inside Moscow, was begun in the twelfth century—long before the city attained importance. In the fifteenth century, under Ivan III, Moscow became supreme over much of Russia. Ivan, the first to call himself Czar, married Sophia, the ward of Pope Sixtus of Rome. In the fresco at right, Sophia and Ivan accept her dowry from Sixtus.

A LA VIEILLE RUSSIE, NEW

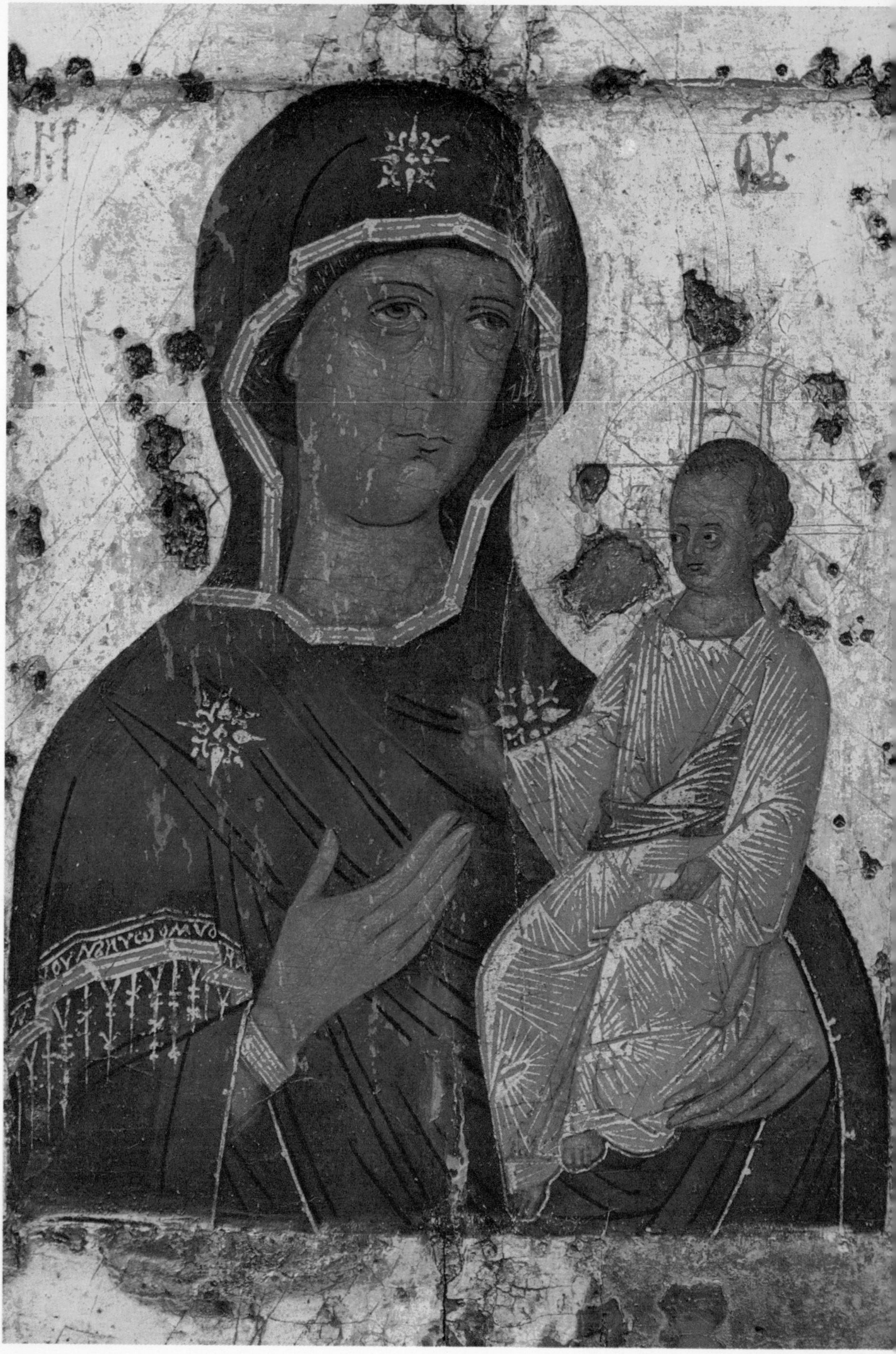

the first Russian ruler who was crowned as Czar.

Ivan was not born terrible. Destiny made him terrible. He achieved great things for Russia and he brought Russia to ruin. He began as a bright, well-intentioned, but unhappy boy and he ended as a mad, evil, unhappy old man.

Ivan was three when his father, Vasily, died. After his mother died too, probably from poison, Ivan was alone. The boyars seized the chance to regain their former power. They imprisoned Ivan's nurse and assassinated her brother, an official who might have protected the boy. Ivan's only companions were his dim-witted brother George and a monk, Sylvester, who tutored both of them. On great occasions palace servants robed Ivan in the splendorous garb of a grand prince and the boyars groveled before him. The rest of the time Ivan and his brother were treated like the children of beggars. "We were badly clothed, we were cold and hungry," Ivan recalled afterward. Boyars strolled about the palace helping themselves to the crown jewels and once one of them put his feet on the royal bed. Spies watched the boys to prevent dangerous friendships; only Sylvester, a servant named Adashev, and some lads who tended the kennels were allowed to talk to them. Sometimes, however, Ivan managed to play with young Prince Kurbsky, the son of a boyar, and a friend who was to have an important role in Ivan's later life.

The boyars, themselves divided by murderous jealousies, were the real rulers. "They wandered everywhere," Ivan remembered, "from palaces to the different villages, exacting fines from the people, making slaves of dignitaries, raising their own slaves to be dignitaries."

By the time he reached his teens, Ivan had had enough. His mind filled with learning by the monk, his heart filled with hatred of the boyars, his face already bearded, he declared his intention to rule and to wed. He began by seating himself on his throne in rich royal garments and announcing to the assembled boyars that he was ordering the arrest of Andrew Shuisky, head of the most important boyar family (and, like himself, a descendant of Rurik). Shuisky fled from the palace. The kennel keepers caught him and killed him. It was more of a warning than Ivan had intended. Frightened, the boyars permitted him to be

André Roubliev, Russia's greatest icon painter of the fourteenth and fifteenth centuries, is seen above at work in Moscow's Androniev Monastery. One of his works was The Virgin of Smolensk, *painted on wood (left).*

crowned, as he demanded, Czar and Autocrat of all Rus. He chose for his bride a pretty young girl, Anastasia Kochkin, from the Romanov clan, which had held aloof from the quarreling boyars.

Ivan began well. He had Sylvester and Adashev to advise him. He had Anastasia, his "little heifer," to soothe his fits of temper. To bring order into the chaos that Muscovy had become, he instituted reforms. The first was the establishment of a legislature which eased the peasants' enslaving burden of taxation. Then he permitted towns and villages to choose their own officials. And he limited the holdings of the monasteries, which had become oppressive landlords controlling a third of the soil.

Organizing an army that was modern for its time, he began to attack and break up the remains of the Golden Horde. He conquered the Tatar Khanate of Kazan, between Muscovy and the Urals, and then the Khanate of Astrakhan. To the southeast the Khanate of Crimea survived. But, protected by a line of forts that Ivan built, Mus-

Antiquities of the Russian Empire, SOLNTSEV, 1849-53

Aristocratic boyars, such as these, were in virtual control of Russia when Ivan IV was a boy. But at the age of sixteen he crowned himself Czar of all Russia and asserted his supremacy by vastly restricting the powers of the rebellious boyars.

covite hunters, trappers, cattlemen, and farmers flooded eastward and southeastward onto the steppes, just as American pioneers moved onto the western prairies centuries later. When the Tatars raided the settlements, bands of frontiersmen called Cossacks (from the Tatar word *kazak*, meaning "free adventurer") fought them off. The Cossacks proved so useful that some of the bands were enlisted as paid auxiliaries in the army, though they accepted no discipline they did not vote to impose upon themselves.

With settlers, army, and Cossacks, Ivan was transforming Muscovy into an empire.

Now he had a fateful choice to make. Should he drive into Crimea and wipe out the Tatar menace forever or should he turn west and fight to open doors into Europe for backward Muscovy?

Prince Kurbsky, who had joined Sylvester and Adashev in the little council of Ivan's friends and advisers, argued for the Crimea. So did Adashev. Had Ivan listened, the Crimean Tatars could not have burned Moscow to the

The Russia of Ivan IV is outlined in the sixteenth-century map below. A likeness of Ivan seated on his throne adorns the upper left corner of the map. The size of Ivan's Russia is compared with that of modern Russia on the map above.

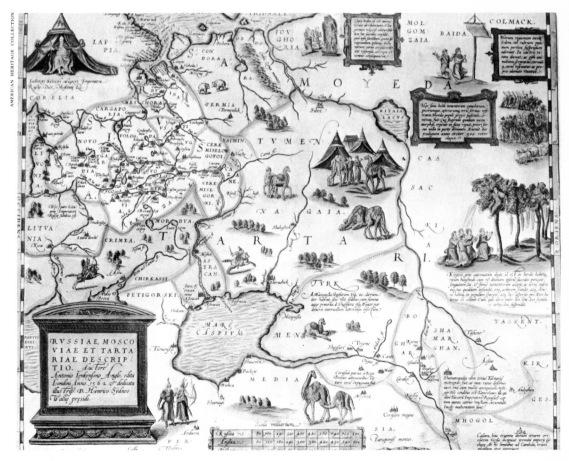

57

ground, as they were to do later in his reign.

But Ivan, with good reason, chose the west. The ports of Riga and Reval on the Baltic Sea were ruled by the Livonian Knights, or Brothers of the Sword, a military monastic order blessed by the pope. If Ivan could take Riga and Reval from them, he could batter down the invisible wall that the Livonians, the Poles, and the Swedes had erected to restrict Muscovy's trade. The wall kept orthodox Muscovy apart from Europe's teachers and engineers, and Ivan determined to destroy it.

Ivan's vision was farsighted. His timing was disastrous. He had barely begun to fight the Livonians when his cherished Anastasia died, leaving him two young sons, Ivan and a simpleton named Fedor. "They have taken my little heifer from me," Ivan cried. The fears and suspicions of his boyhood overwhelmed him. Anastasia was not there to reason with him. Darkly, he decided that his friends and councilors had poisoned his wife. He hustled Sylvester off to exile in a remote monastery, sent Adashev to fight and die in Livonia, and dismissed Kurbsky as an adviser. The war began to go badly: Lithuania, Poland, and Sweden allied themselves with the Livonian Knights, and Ivan's armies were no longer victorious. In a fury, Ivan imprisoned or executed beaten generals. The war had raged for six years when Prince Kurbsky, who was proving himself one of the best of Ivan's commanders, met defeat at Lithuanian hands. Disillusioned with Ivan, unwilling to return home to unjust punishment, Kurbsky joined the Lithuanians.

If Kurbsky could betray him, whom could he trust? Ivan began to suspect everyone and to see plotters everywhere, especially among the boyars. Cunningly he devised a scheme to foil his imagined enemies.

He slipped out of Moscow to a small town forty-five miles away and sent back word that boyar treachery was forcing him to abdicate. As he expected, the people of Muscovy begged him to return. He agreed to do so only if he could have absolute power to rule, to punish, and to protect himself. The people assented.

The great danger of absolute power, greater even than the fact that it corrupts its possessors, is that it may fall into the hands of a madman. Ivan, soon to become known

During Ivan's reign Russia preserved her link with Europe through trade. The German miniature at left shows the teeming port of Hamburg, where Russian grain, honey, and furs were exchanged for metalware, silks, and linens.

throughout Russia as the Terrible, was going mad.

On the pretext of protecting himself, he enlisted a strange six-thousand-man bodyguard of minor landowners, commoners, German prisoners of war, foreign adventurers, and boyars who were willing to give up their loyalty to the boyar class. Perhaps to mock the early influence of the good monk Sylvester, he dressed them in black monkish robes and called them "brethren." But they were devoted to looting and terrorizing the countryside rather than to religion. In the small town where he had pretended to abdicate, Ivan presided over his monastery of murderers as an evil abbot, drinking, torturing, and carefully keeping lists of the victims so he could order prayers for their souls. No one was safe. When the Metropolitan, or Archbishop, of Moscow protested, Ivan had him strangled by one of his "monks"—or *oprichniki*, as they were called. And when Ivan began to run short of victims, he tortured and killed *oprichniki* too.

In his obsession to destroy the boyar class, he made half of Russia's land his own property; over the remaining half of the land he set up a rival "czar" who had no real power. In his insane suspicion he attacked Novgorod with an army, pillaging, torturing and killing for weeks, until

In manner and dress, Czar Ivan IV (right) presented the perfect image of an all-powerful Russian dictator. Throughout his long reign he fought hard to expand his empire. In 1554, to celebrate his victories over the Tatars, he ordered the construction of the majestic and beautiful Church of St. Basil the Blessed (left), which stands today in Moscow's Red Square.

corpses filled the river Volkhov to overflowing. In his longing for the love he had got only from Anastasia, he married and discarded six wives.

Disaster was descending on the Muscovy to which Ivan had given such a good start. The war in the west, which dragged on for twenty-five years, was being lost, and in a vain attempt to salvage it by rallying support, Ivan had to dissolve his *oprichniki* and give back the lands he had seized. Crimean Tatars swooped down on Moscow and burned everything but the Kremlin. Cossacks (many of them Tatars themselves), who did not care whom they fought, raided and pillaged Ivan's cities. Peasants, displaced by the chaos, fled toward the new territories opening up in Siberia, beyond the Urals, and their flight threatened to depopulate Muscovy.

Aging, weary, wasted, Ivan let authority slip from his hands. He could only hope that his elder son would do better than he had done. But Ivan had not yet done his most terrible deed. Two years before his death, in a wild rage, he struck the boy fatally with a heavy staff. Three days later a grief-stricken, remorseful Czar saw young Ivan die. Poor simple-minded Fedor became the heir to the throne, the last of the House of Rurik to rule in Russia.

Absolute power, of which Genghis Khan too had dreamed, had destroyed Ivan the Terrible and his family; it had almost destroyed his country.

Ivan's cruelty is expressed above in an ancient woodcut. Astride a horse, his executioners around him, he holds a lance impaling a human head. Behind him are people he has sentenced to death. The painting at right shows a grief-stricken Ivan embracing his son—whom he has struck down in a rage.

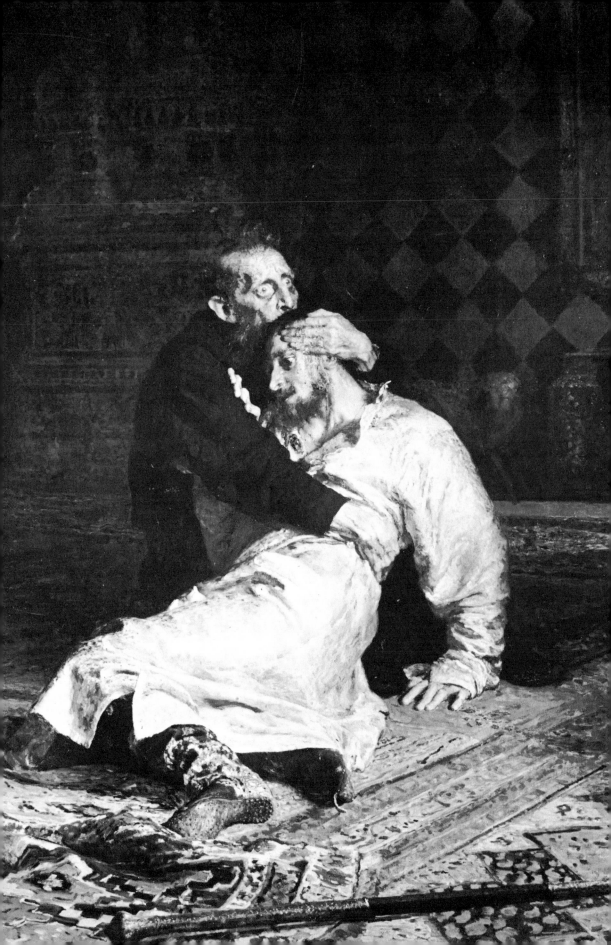

IV

THE PRETENDERS

Ivan the Terrible's delayed legacy to Russia was a series of fantastic and mysterious events which Russians call the Time of the Troubles. About one of the enigmatic figures who emerged to rule Russia in this period of supreme agony a splendid opera has been written, *Boris Godunov*. But even Russia seems a stage hardly big enough to encompass all the incredible characters involved in the drama that was a prelude to the longer drama of Peter the Great.

What brought about the Time of the Troubles was the tragic inadequacy of Fedor, who was as careless of power as the boyars were greedy for it. Twenty-seven when he came to the throne, he shuffled, he squeaked, and he perpetually wore an idiot's smile; to pass the time he played with his scepter and pulled the ropes of church bells. Yet there was no one to be czar in his place. His two-year-old half-brother, Prince Dmitry, was the son of Ivan the Terrible's last wife, but the Church did not recognize that marriage, so Dmitry did not count. At least not yet. In fact, the little boy would not count until he was dead.

Into the power vacuum created by Fedor's weakness stepped Boris Godunov, handsome brother of Czar Fedor's wife. At first he ruled while Fedor reigned; after Fedor's death, he both ruled and reigned as elected czar. Of Tatar descent and a son-in-law of the worst of Ivan the Terrible's *oprichniki*, Boris was an able man with a vast respect for learning. He determined to govern justly and wisely. Admiringly, the English envoy Jerome Horsey reported to Queen Elizabeth "Every man living in peace, enjoying and knowing his own; good officers placed, justice administered everywhere." But he added: "Yet, God hath a great plague in store for this people." His words were prophetic.

Fedor I, last of the House of Rurik

Peasants storm a monastery in this painting of a seventeenth-century uprising. They are armed with scythes and pruning knives and a few have rifles.

The Church, always conservative, balked at Boris' proposal to bring in Western teachers, and the young noblemen whom Boris had sent abroad to study never returned home. His boyar enemies, whom Boris declined to execute, plotted against him in exile. Three successive years of famine, in 1601, 1602, and 1603, drove the peasants, despite Boris' relief efforts, to brigandage and cannibalism. Little Prince Dmitry, living in a remote town with his mother, died mysteriously of a knife wound. And the boyar families, never reconciled to their loss of power, began to whisper that Boris had had the boy murdered. The tales grew with the telling: Boris, it was said, had also murdered Czar Fedor's infant daughter—and Fedor himself.

Was the well-intentioned Boris really a dark assassin? We shall never know. But fear born of the conspiracies against him led him to install spies in the houses of all potential foes, thus inaugurating the secret police system that has plagued Russia ever since.

Meanwhile, little Dmitry, twelve years after his death, was becoming more important than he had been in life, for a mysterious young man arose to proclaim that he was Dmitry and the rightful czar. Boris' hired killers, he explained, had stabbed the wrong boy. Perhaps the false Dmitry had been brainwashed or hypnotized by Boris' princely enemies. But, like others of the many pretenders who have appeared in Russian history, he believed his own story. So did thousands of Russians who acclaimed him as he marched on Moscow with a tattered army of rebellious troops, runaway serfs, Poles and Cossacks. The real Dmitry's mother believed him too—or so she said upon emerging from a nunnery, eager to return to the Kremlin.

Perhaps Boris could have beaten off the false Dmitry. He was preparing to do so when he died suddenly, at the age of fifty-three, in April, 1605. A mob incited by the boyars invaded the Kremlin and murdered Boris' son and heir as well as Boris' wife.

The false Dmitry assumed the throne as czar and took a Polish wife, Marina, as czarina. But the men who had trained him had done their job too well. Intelligent, oriented to Western ideas, and convinced that he ruled by right, Dmitry quickly infuriated the very princes who had created him by refusing to be their puppet. Once again a boyar-incited mob invaded the Kremlin. Marina escaped, but Dmitry—whoever he really was—perished.

Yet with his death the Time of the Troubles was not over; it was merely beginning. Prince Vasily Shuisky, one

Czar Boris Godunov

of the plotters who had brought Dmitry to the throne and then helped to depose him, seized the royal power. Throughout the country revolt flared against him. A runaway serf named Ivan Bolotnikov raised the lower classes against their masters, urging them to pillage, burn, torture, and murder. Then another false Dmitry appeared. And though this second Dmitry was a lout nicknamed the Thief of Tushino who bore no resemblance to the first pretender, Marina embraced him as her long-lost husband. Supporters flocked to his standard, and troops sent unofficially by the king of Poland joined the Thief in besieging Moscow.

To help defeat the Polish troops, Sweden joined the fight on Czar Vasily Shuisky's side, and the desperate czar paid Sweden for its help with the Russian-held province of Karelia. Poland's King Sigismund, eying Russia's throne for himself or his young son, responded by officially declaring war on Russia. In the chaos, a group of military men dethroned Shuisky. The Thief of Tushino was mur-

BOTH: *Antient and Present State of Muscovy*, CRULL, 1698

Each of these mysterious men pretended to be Dmitry, second son of Ivan the Terrible. The First Dmitry, as he has come to be called, is at left; he reigned for two years, but proved too capable to be a tool of the boyars.

THE COSSACKS

Galloping across the pages of Russian history, the Cossacks have fought for freedom and for tyranny. Traditionally they were loose bands of pirates and freebooters who lived in independent colonies on Russia's major rivers (left). During the Time of the Troubles they helped to put a new czar into the Kremlin. The Don Cossacks (who carried lances like the cavalryman at right below) revolted repeatedly against the spreading power of the Russian state, and they were joined by thousands of other oppressed Russians. After Catherine the Great and under the later emperors, the Cossacks lost their independence and came to be used in regular army units. But whether lined up for inspection (below) or charging into battle (right), they remained proud, fierce, and ruthless.

69

dered by one of his own followers. And the twice-widowed Marina ran off with a Cossack chieftain. Russia was czarless, leaderless, and torn by the hatreds and rivalries of princes, military men, Cossacks, landowning gentry, and peasants. The war-racked country was carved up like a steer. The Poles took Moscow, Smolensk, and the southwest; the Swedes seized Novgorod and the northwest.

But Russian patriotism seems to rise highest when Russia's national fortunes are at their lowest. From the Church, whose monks had fought bravely against the invaders, came calls for national unity. From a butcher and cattle merchant named Kuzma Minin, who was mayor of Nizhny-Novgorod, came pleas for money to raise a fighting force to drive out the foreigners. From a local prince named Dmitry Pozharsky came military skill.

The wildest group of Cossacks were the Zaporogs, who lived in island fortresses in the Dnieper. The Russian artist Repin painted this scene of the Zaporog Cossacks writing an insulting letter to a foreign ruler.

The peasants and serfs supplied most of the raw manpower. As bands of fighting men swept through the countryside these ragged people of the lower classes would join them—hoping that somehow their stomachs would be filled and their livelihood improved. The peasants' piety let them believe anyone who called on them in the name of Russia and the Church. The serfs, who were technically as free as the peasants but who were in fact bound to the landowners by indebtedness, left the estates in vast numbers, seeking freedom and a new beginning.

As King Sigismund hurried reinforcements to the Polish garrison occupying Moscow, and the Kremlin itself, Pozharsky marched on the capital in July, 1612, with a popular army. He found Cossacks already besieging the city. But the Cossacks had their own ideas about Russia's future: they wanted the whole country to be governed as democratically as they governed themselves, and they desired no help from a prince. Pozharsky and the Cossacks argued. At that moment the Polish reinforcements arrived and attacked. But rather than yield in an argument, the Cossacks quit the siege and stood aloof while Pozharsky and his troops fought the Poles. It was only at the last minute that the Cossacks joined the battle and helped the prince capture part of the city. Then they went on to besiege the Kremlin.

Four days later the starving Poles surrendered. The liberation of Russia was under way and the Time of the Troubles was almost over. In January, 1613, a *zemsky sobor*, or assembly of the land, in which every class including the peasantry took part, met to choose a czar. It selected sixteen-year-old Michael Romanov, a distant relative of Ivan the Terrible's beloved "little heifer," Anastasia.

Czar Michael Romanov was not to be envied. The land he was to rule was as bankrupt and desolate as the land that Ivan the Terrible had left to Fedor, and neither Michael nor his son Alexis, who succeeded him, could do much to change it.

Nevertheless, it had been changed in one way. Russia had been liberated by merchants like Kuzma Minin and by provincial landowning gentry like Pozharsky, not by Cossacks or old-line boyars or rebelling peasants. Cossacks and boyars would linger to make trouble and peasant uprisings would continue, but these elements had lost their chance to dominate the country. Until the present century, Russia would be controlled by the landowners, who gave the crown to the Romanovs and their burdens to the serfs.

BOTH: *Sources for Russian Iconography.* ROVINSKI, 1884–90

A great Cossack hero was Hetman, or General, Sahaydachny (above) who rampaged through the Crimea (top) and into the Ukraine during the turbulent Time of the Troubles.

V

PETER THE GREAT

Of all the extraordinary men who have ruled Russia, none is more fascinating than Michael Romanov's grandson, Peter the Great. Almost seven feet tall, he was broad-shouldered and big-muscled, handsome and blue-eyed, furiously energetic, and prodigiously strong. Peter commanded the bodies and souls of millions of people, but he himself wielded an axe to help build a navy, and even served as a corporal in his own army. With palaces to loll in, he often lived content in a two-room shack; with Russian nobles to fawn on him, he sought the company of foreigners and commoners who talked back. Part hero and part ogre, he could be as cruel as Ivan the Terrible, but his cruelty was intended to flog a lazy, ignorant, and corrupt Russia into greatness.

Peter was the royal family's fourteenth child. Yet his birth in the Kremlin on May 30, 1672, touched off far more excited rejoicing than a fourteenth child generally merits. As the firstborn of Czar Alexis' cherished young second wife, and as a lusty male, the baby was a more attractive heir to the throne than Peter's two sickly, surviving half-brothers, Fedor and Ivan.

Six years after their weak but well-meaning father died, Fedor also died. Peter, who was ten but looked a rugged sixteen, was proclaimed czar by the Patriarch of the Church and by a group of boyars. Yet a plot was afoot to make Ivan czar and his sister Sophia regent. The plain-faced, twenty-five-year-old Sophia planned to bring about a palace revolution by stirring up the people against Peter's mother and her trusted councilor, Artemon Matveev.

Majestically turned out in battle armor, Peter the Great enjoys a rare moment of serenity at left. In life he seldom stood still; courtiers had to run to keep up with him. His grandfather, Czar Michael Romanov, is above.

Carefully, Sophia prepared her plot, sending secret agents to whisper fantastic tales in the court and among the *Streltsy*, the Moscow Guard regiments. The agents slyly suggested that Peter's mother, Natalya Naryshkin, had poisoned Fedor and was now planning to harm Ivan. They also hinted that Natalya and Matveev were going to betray the country to foreigners.

Then Sophia moved. It was the morning of May 15, 1682. As Moscow began bustling with the day's business, two horsemen clamored through the streets, shouting that Matveev and the Naryshkin family had strangled Ivan.

The *Streltsy* seized their weapons and started toward the

This nineteenth-century engraving depicts one of the Streltsy *raids on the royal palace. Natalya is pictured shielding her young son Peter from a guardsman's attack.*

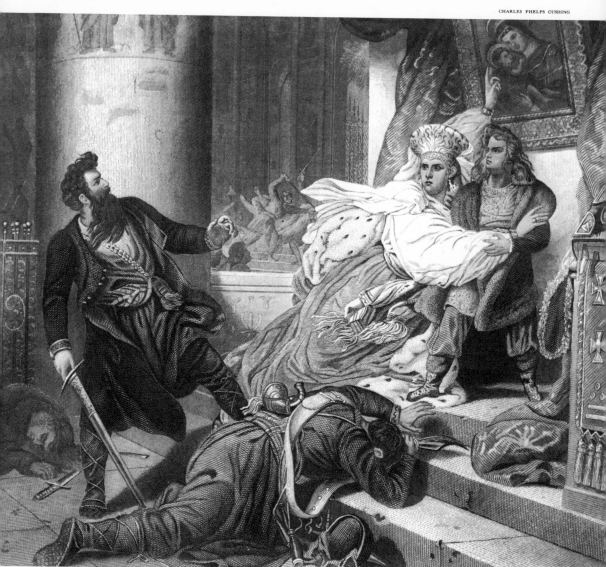

Fedor, shown above, was czar before Peter, seen below as a child.

Kremlin. Civilians snatched up sticks and stones. Pouring into the muddy square before the Granovitaya Palace where Natalya and the two boys lived, the mob screamed, "Hand over Matveev! Hand over the Naryshkins!" In minutes they would be inside. Calmly, Matveev advised Natalya to go out on the Red Balcony above the square and show Peter and Ivan to the frenzied throng. Terrified, a tragic figure in widow's black, Natalya stepped through a window with the huge Peter and the spindly Ivan at her side. Fright choked her. Matveev strode onto the balcony. "Who lied to you?" he shouted. "Here is Czar Peter well and happy. Here is the Czarevich Ivan. Nobody has harmed him. Who lied to you?" Then he reminded the *Streltsy* that they had always been brave soldiers and good patriots. They must not blacken their noble record now.

The guardsmen shifted uneasily. Then young Prince Dolgoruky, whose father commanded the *Streltsy*, raced down the staircase into the square. Flailing his whip, he cursed the soldiers: if his father were not ill, they would not dare behave thus. The *Streltsy*, fending off his whip, surged toward him. He backed up the staircase, sword drawn. The soldiers pursued him, caught him at the top, held him high in the air, and threw him over the railing onto the pikes of their comrades below. Speechless, Peter and Ivan clung to Natalya. The *Streltsy* now turned on Matveev. Natalya, suddenly courageous, threw her frail arms around the old man. But they pulled her away, brushed aside Peter and a sobbing Ivan, and tossed Matveev to the mob. For three days the *Streltsy* stormed repeatedly through the palace, hunting down and killing Natalya's kinsmen. Sophia had won—for the time.

All Peter's life a twitch contorted his handsome face as a result of that dreadful day. All his life he hated Moscow, the scene of his terror. All his life he hated the ignorance that turned good men so easily into frenzied killers. And all his life he applied his tremendous strength and energy to an effort to transform the Russia in which such things could happen.

The immediate result of Sophia's plot was that Peter and Ivan became czars reigning jointly under Sophia's regency. They sat side by side on a double throne while Sophia prompted them in whispers from behind a curtain. And it must be said that Sophia ruled wisely and well, at least at first, and kept beheadings to a minimum. She treated Peter fairly enough, bestowing on him noble playmates and servants and letting him do as he wished. But, taking no chances, she allowed him and his mother to live in the village of Preobrazhenskoe on the outskirts of Moscow. A shrewd boy, aware that his position was precarious, Peter decided he needed a bodyguard. So he rounded up noble young friends, village boys, and peasants and drilled them tirelessly in the fields, arming them with weapons from the royal arsenal. At first, wooden cannons that fired squashy fruits and vegetables satisfied him. Then he demanded, and got, real cannon. When his "men" were, in his boyish judgment, well enough trained, he divided them into two regiments and pitted them against each other in ferocious sham battles that produced real casualties. With Peter, only courage and ability counted: one of his best friends was a groom's son named Menshikov, who became a lifelong adviser.

Peter and his "troops" soldiered almost incessantly. When Peter's tutor called him to his lessons, Peter tethered him to a tree, with a bottle of liquor to keep him quiet, and went on fighting his mock wars. But if he learned little from his tutor, he learned a great deal by himself. He

After the Streltsy *revolt, Peter's half-sister Sophia became regent of Russia in place of his mother. Sophia opposed Peter all her life and ended her days a prisoner in a remote nunnery (left). As a young czar, Peter formed his companions into a mock army which he drilled and led in elaborately staged battle games. In the miniature at right, Peter (top) commands an "army" besieging a fortress. His guns fired nonexplosive, leather-covered cannon balls.*

Sources for Russian Iconography, ROVINSKI, 1884–90

On state occasions, Peter and his half-brother Ivan sat side by side on the royal throne (right). According to gossip, Sophia often hid herself behind the throne to prompt. Peter's skills were many, and his curiosity boundless. To learn more about shipbuilding, he retired to his room to carve a rudder (below).

bought tools and began to acquire skill as a carpenter, a stonemason, a metalsmith, and later as a printer and a dentist: eventually his big hands mastered fifteen trades. He heard about a device called an astrolabe—invented by the ancient Greeks and recently rediscovered—which permitted one to calculate latitude and time of day, and he obtained it from Paris. In Moscow's German Quarter he found a Dutchman named Franz Timmerman who knew how to use the instrument. But to understand it one had to learn arithmetic and geometry. Soon Peter, who could barely write or spell, was doggedly studying arithmetic and geometry. When he had conquered these subjects, he discovered he could calculate the arc of a mortar shell. From the study of artillery fire it was a mere step to the study of fortification, in which a Scot and a Swiss from the German Quarter instructed him. The Western ways of the German Quarter's folk fascinated Peter, and the attraction grew even stronger when one day, while strolling with Timmerman, Peter came upon a trim but unrigged boat in a village barn. It was unlike the flat-bottomed barges of Russia, and it resembled no boat Peter had ever seen. Timmerman explained that it was English and that equipped with sails and a mast it could make good time against the wind.

Within weeks Peter was learning to sail the foreign boat against the wind. And he realized for the first time how the British and the Dutch were able to command the seas and to trade the world over. Then Russia must have ships, and Peter would order them built. But apart from the icy port of Archangel, Russia had only lakes and rivers on which to sail them. Peter decided that Russia must have ice-free ports.

Peter was now nearly seventeen. His boyhood was barely over, but he was a full-grown, huge-limbed giant. And influenced by the bloodiness of the *Streltsy* rebellion, by his play regiments, by the old boat, and by all the amazing things he had learned in the German Quarter, he had already set the course of his whole life—a course that would change Russia's history.

To his mother, Peter's approach to manhood meant only that it was time for him to marry and to forget his dangerous hobbies. Obediently Peter married a pretty, dull young Muscovite named Eudoxia Lopukhina, and went back to sailing his boats. To Sophia, Peter's new manhood signaled danger. No doubt he would want to be czar in fact. But Sophia had no intention of yielding power.

With the help of the *Streltsy*, she could rid herself of Peter and transform herself from regent into czarina. Ivan, who was dim-witted, would not mind.

One midnight in August, 1689, Peter was asleep in Preobrazhenskoe when a messenger from a friend in Moscow rode into the village. The *Streltsy*, he reported, were on their way to murder Peter. Twitching with terror, Peter raced to the stables without pausing to dress. Leaping onto a horse, he galloped some forty miles to the sanctuary of a monastery. The alarm spread quickly. Peter's play regiments mobilized to protect him. Regular troops, shocked at the idea of a plot against the young Czar, hurried to support him. So did a few companies of *Streltsy* who had secretly resented Sophia. Sophia still had powerful backers; the issue was not decided. Peter boldly took the offensive and ordered the arrest of Sophia's most important friends. Frightened, Sophia's troops deserted to Peter. This time Sophia had lost. Protesting furiously, she was shipped off at Peter's orders to the nunnery she had feared. Now Peter was really czar. Ivan could wear the robes. Ivan could sit on the throne to receive ambassadors. Ivan could march in church processionals. Peter had work to do.

This land of Peter's—for with Ivan's death a little later it was all his—was vast. It sprawled from the frozen Arctic regions to the warmth of the Caspian Sea, from the eastern tip of unpeopled Siberia to populous Western Europe. But it was a giant in manacles. In the south, Turks and Tatars held the steppes that bordered the Caspian, and the Turkish fortress at Azov, at the mouth of the Don River, blocked the way to the Black Sea. To the northwest, Sweden, commanding the Baltic provinces, stood as a barrier to the Baltic Sea. Only Archangel on the little White Sea, which was frozen most of the year, opened a narrow Russian door to commerce with the world. In effect, Russia was a great island almost entirely surrounded by land. Worse, Russia was a giant that seemed to enjoy manacles. As backward as it was vast, a country of beggars, of serfs who were virtual slaves, and of a few callous, greedy rich, it neither helped itself nor wanted anyone else to help it. It hated foreigners, for foreigners were Roman Catholics or Protestants and therefore enemies of Russia's Orthodox Church. Learning was suspect, for learning meant foreign ideas, and foreign ideas were dangerous. Czar Peter set out to hack off Russia's manacles, whether Russia wanted them or not. He would open the way to the Black Sea. He would win ports on the Baltic, as Ivan the Terrible had dreamed

Peter traveled extensively to learn Western ways and customs. But at first he traveled in disguise, for he wanted to avoid royal treatment. In Holland he dressed as a peasant (right) and lived in a blacksmith's hut (below). Later, disguised no more, he visited France (at far right) where he met young Louis XV.

*Whether fighting wars or practicing
dentistry (above), Peter was violent.*

of doing. He would educate Russians, as Boris Godunov
had tried to do. He would make Russia as modern as any
Western land, but he would keep it Russian.

He began with the Turkish fort at Azov. In 1695 the
play regiments, the *Streltsy*, and regular troops trained by
foreigners, in all an army of some thirty thousand men,
left Moscow. With them went twenty-two-year-old Corporal Peter Alexeev, bombardier in the Preobrazhensky
Regiment, which had been one of Peter's play regiments.
The corporal was Czar Peter, serving as a common soldier
to avoid the bowing and scraping that people felt he de-
served as a monarch. The seven months' adventure was
disastrous. The Turks repulsed the land attacks of Peter's
army with heavy casualties, and the Russians were not
equipped to attack by water. Peter marched home with a
beaten army. Characteristically, he decided that next year
he would do better; next year he would have a fleet. But
time was short. Peter sent to Austria and Prussia for military engineers. He rounded up every foreigner in Russia
who knew anything about building boats and barges. He
impressed many thousands of peasants as laborers to chop
trees and hew timbers. At Voronezh he set up riverside
shipyards where axes rang and hammers thudded day and
night while boatwrights shaped a fleet of warships, galleys,
fireships, and hundreds of barges. Mightiest of all the
workmen was a skilled carpenter who lived in a two-room
shack—Czar Peter. And when the fleet sailed downriver in
support of an army of seventy thousand men, one eight-
vessel squadron was commanded by a captain who had
built his flagship himself, Czar Peter.

Azov fell. The southern steppes and the mouth of the
Don were in Russian hands.

Rarely in history has the capture of a single fortress had
such tremendous consequences. The fall of Azov in 1696
allowed Peter to turn to Western Europe with the expectation that he would be regarded by other kings and princes
as master of an expanding and powerful state. With the
spring thaw of 1697, a few months after Azov's conquest,
a huge diplomatic mission set out from Moscow for a tour of
Europe. Its 250 members included Russian officials, foreign
advisers, some sixtyscore young Russian nobles whose
parents worried about their exposure to the wicked West,
and a huge young Russian sailor who called himself Peter
Mikhailov and who was, of course, Czar Peter.

The mission had two purposes. The first was to seek
allies for a massive Russian effort to destroy the whole

РАСКОЛЬНІКЪ ГОВОРИТЪ
СЛУШЇЙ ЦЫРЮЛЬНИКЪ
Я БОРОДЫ СТРИЙЪ НЕ
ХОЦУ ВОТЪ ГЛЕДИ Я НА
ТЕБЯ СКОРО КАРАУЛЪ ЗАКРЇУ

ЦЫРЮЛНІЙКЪ ХО
ЧЕТЪ РАСКОЛЬНИКУ
БОРОДУ СТРИЧЪ •

In this cheery cartoon Peter is snipping off the beard of an unhappy boyar.
Peter returned from Europe determined to change Russia's backward society.

83

great Turkish empire—then Russia would dot the Black Sea with ports and perhaps make even Constantinople Russian. The second was to introduce the touring Russians, and especially Peter, to Western ways. The mission found no one ready to help take on Turkey, but it did educate Peter and his entourage, who at the outset, as one European courtier put it, were merely "baptized bears." Peter learned more than just table manners. In Germany he mastered gunnery. In the Netherlands he got jobs for himself and some companions in a shipyard and mastered shipbuilding. He studied anatomy and engraving, hired hundreds of technicians, artisans, and naval men to work in Russia, and contracted for the printing of technical books in Russian. In England he studied everything from coinage to naval

A Streltsy *attempt to topple Peter's government set off a wave of executions in 1698. Before St. Basil's Church in Red Square, the* Streltsy *were led to the gallows.*

tactics, engaged engineers to design canals to link Russian rivers, and hired instructors to teach Russians mathematics and navigation.

The first day of his return home, Peter began reforming Russia with a pair of scissors. He had been away eighteen months. At the news that he was back, the great and the humble streamed from Moscow to prostrate themselves before him in his hut at Preobrazhenskoe, where he had spent the night among his play regiments. Peter embraced his welcomers. Then, with a barberlike flourish, he produced shears and snipped off beard after beard.

To Peter the beard represented Russian backwardness, and for the rest of his life he continued, figuratively, to snip off Russian beards. Because they looked Oriental, he outlawed the long coats that Muscovites had worn for centuries. He replaced the calendar that counted the years since "the creation of the world" with the Julian calendar based on the birth of Christ. He opened technical schools and he established Russia's first newspaper. He reorganized the government and the army, built a real navy, and fostered the establishment of new industries. He set thousands of men to work building a new capital to be called St. Petersburg, which would be a western seaport and which would replace the Moscow he hated.

But inexperience raised tremendous obstacles. The site of the new capital was a fogbound swamp, and so many men died working on the city that St. Petersburg has been called the city built on bones. Thousands more died working on the city's waterways, but the canals were too shallow for ocean-going vessels. The industries were state managed, as they are in Russia today. This discouraged private investment and slowed the country's economic growth.

Peter had to fight opposition as well as inexperience. Russians considered their beards "passports to heaven" and furiously protested against cutting them off; students in the new schools were reluctant to learn. Again and again opposition flared against Peter's reforms, and he crushed it as ruthlessly as he drove the canal diggers and the builders of St. Petersburg. When the *Streltsy* plotted to overthrow him and replace him with Sophia, he personally tortured and executed the ringleaders. He had some of them broken

STATE TRETYAKOV GALLERY, MOSCOW

STATE TRETYAKOV GALLERY, MOSCOW

OVERLEAF: *For Peter, who became the father of the Russian navy, nothing was so exciting as ships and the sea. Visiting Amsterdam, the red-coated Czar stood tall in a sloop to watch Dutch cargo ships sail into the harbor.*

NATIONAL MARITIME MUSEUM, GREENWICH

85

on the wheel, the rest beheaded or hanged. Energy and cruelty together won for Peter much of what he wanted. St. Petersburg eventually became a splendid city. The navy eventually won a great victory over Sweden. The technical schools eventually ranked with the world's best. The canals eventually floated great quantities of cargo.

Peter's year and a half abroad had another result quite as important as his internal reforms. Although he had found no power interested in joining him in destroying the Turkish empire, he did find Frederick Augustus, Elector of Saxony and King of Poland, and King Christian of Denmark eager to war upon Sweden. The idea attracted Peter: Sweden was Russia's ancient enemy, Sweden was the barrier to the Baltic. Furthermore, it looked like an easy war. Sweden's King Charles XII was a boy of eighteen, a huge, wild lad who enjoyed street fights, rode horses to death, and had no experience as ruler or soldier. Enlisting Poland and Denmark as allies, Peter began the war just as he had first marched against Azov, with more enthusiasm than preparation. Professing friendship for Sweden until the moment of attack, he hurled thirty-five thousand men against Charles' army in the summer of 1700. The untried Charles, who was to prove one of the great generals of all time, sent Peter fleeing, crushed Denmark in no time, and then turned to Poland. But Peter, like Russian generals before and after him, profited by initial defeat. While Charles floundered in the Polish mud, Peter retrained and rebuilt his army, then counterattacked.

The war raged on and on. Digging canals, building St. Petersburg, crushing opposition, and fighting a war, all simultaneously, Peter stripped the country of men, of food, of money, of every resource. Church bells were melted down to make cannon. Draftees were dragged into the army for twenty-five years service, but few lived that long. Everything was taxed, even coffins, and Peter offered huge prizes to the inventors of new taxes.

In the ninth year of the war, Peter and Charles met in a decisive battle at Poltava in southern Russia. It was a conflict of giants. Charles, wounded before the battle, directed his troops from a stretcher until a cannon ball threw him to the ground, then he had himself borne on an improvised litter of poles. Peter galloped about the field, undaunted by bullets that knocked off his hat and shattered the crucifix on his chest. Peter won; Charles fled to Turkey. But the "short war" lasted another twelve years, and when it ended, Peter was the only one left of the four rulers who

Encounters between Peter (seated) and his son Alexis were rare. The young man hated Peter and opposed his new ideas. Eventually Alexis was tried and sentenced to death.

At the battle of Poltava in 1709 the Swedes were defeated and their king, Charles XII, was wounded. In the drawing below, he is shown directing his army from a stretcher.

had begun it. Its cost in lives, in suffering, in resources, had been incalculable. But Sweden's Baltic lands—Ingria, Estonia, and Latvia—were now Russian. Peter had won the western window to the world of which he had dreamed when he first sailed the little boat he had found in the barn. And in recognition of his victory he was proclaimed Emperor of Russia.

Now Peter was almost fifty. Who would succeed him? His only living son, Alexis, hated him as a betrayer of Russian tradition, and despite Peter's efforts to win his affection, Alexis plotted against him. And when the young man's plots with Peter's despised "gray beards" of the Church were discovered, Alexis provoked an international scandal by fleeing to Vienna to put himself under the protection of the emperor of Austria. He was returned to Russia after long and involved diplomatic exchanges. Then, with the brutal firmness he had shown all his life to those who opposed Russia's advancement, Peter had his son tortured and tried for treason. After a torment of deliberation, the judges sentenced Alexis to death. But fate spared Peter the burden of beheading his own son. Alexis died of fright and exhaustion in his prison cell.

As scornful as ever of his people's prejudices, Peter devised one last shock for the Russians who had disapproved of his ways ever since he first began consorting with the foreigners of the German Quarter. Long ago he had replaced his wife with a Lithuanian servant girl named Catherine Skavronskaya. She had shared his huts and his hardships, had cared for him tenderly, had soothed his rages, and had borne him eleven children. Unlettered, she was a woman of charm, beauty, and wisdom. But the Russians had never accepted her. Now Peter defiantly crowned her as his empress.

Though he was still driving himself as he had always driven his people, death was not far off. For Peter the Great the end was a fitting one. On January 28, 1725, in his palace in the city of St. Petersburg, which he had conjured out of a swamp, Peter died of an illness contracted when he plunged into a winter sea to rescue some drowning sailors.

And the Russia that had hated him wept.

Near Cape Hango in the Baltic Sea, Peter's many-oared galleys attacked and routed the Swedish fleet that barred the way to the Swedish mainland. This Russian victory in 1714 was the first major success of Peter's new navy.

92

IMPERIAL ST. PETERSBURG

Peter the Great's most dazzling legacy to Russia was St. Petersburg. Even today, when his dream of a westward-facing port city at the swampy mouth of the Neva River has been forgotten and the city has been renamed Leningrad, it has a style and a magnificence that can be found nowhere else in Russia. With his enormous energy, Peter pushed forward plans for a network of canals and islands that would rival those of Amsterdam and Venice. Although that scheme failed after thousands died trying to drain the swamps, Peter did succeed in making St. Petersburg imperial in appearance and bright with water. At left is an 1815 engraving showing the Great Bridge across the Neva. Peter also made his capital look unlike old Moscow. His own residence, Peterhof (whose fountains are shown at left below), is built like a Roman villa, and the Winter Palace (below) carries out this theme. Symbolic of St. Petersburg is the equestrian statue above showing Peter's horse crushing a snake. The snake is the spirit of Russian backwardness.

VI

CATHERINE, EMPRESS OF ALL THE RUSSIAS

A small band of Guard officers was about to leave Moscow on the night of November 24, 1741. They were going to fight the Swedes, who were attempting to take back the territory won by the forces of Peter the Great. But they knew that it was not the Swedes who were at the heart of Russia's troubles; it was royal incompetence.

Peter the Great had decreed that each czar was to name his own successor, but he himself had been unable to choose one. His last words on his deathbed were, "Give every-thing to . . ." He never finished the sentence. Hence, the crown had been passed to his heirs and those of his idiotic half-brother, Ivan. Ivan's heirs, German by birth and up-bringing as a result of royal marriages, had been ruling for eleven years. By their laziness and their dependence on foreign advisers they had lost the commanding position that Peter had achieved for Russia in Europe. Now, the Imperial Guard, which had been created by Peter from his old play troops to replace the mutinous *Streltsy*, had had enough. It was time to act.

They had no doubt about who was the best choice for the throne: Peter's lusty, big-framed, but beautiful daughter, Elizabeth. They knew her, for she liked to drink with them in their barracks and she had had a Guard sergeant as her sweetheart—before her ruling German cousins had sent him to Siberia with his tongue cut out. Visiting her surreptitiously just before their scheduled departure, the Guard officers urged Elizabeth to seize the throne. When

Incredibly proud of her good looks and her fine dresses, Empress Elizabeth (above) lacked the driving will that made Catherine II great. Catherine (right) became empress by deposing her husband, who was Elizabeth's heir.

94

she had heard them out, she donned a cuirass, picked up a crucifix, and rode off with the soldiers to the quarters of the Preobrazhensky Regiment. The Guard swore allegiance to her. Torches held high, they paraded behind her to the Winter Palace where the baby emperor, Ivan VI, lived. Regent for Ivan was his mother, Anne, a slothful shrew who was Peter the Great's grandniece. Elizabeth strode into Anne's room, shook her and said, "Time to get up, Sister." The Guard arrested Anne's advisers. Elizabeth hustled Anne and her family off to exile—except for the innocent child whom she fondled and kissed before the soldiers took him away to a secret cell in the fortress of Schlüsselberg.

Had Elizabeth been born to England's throne and raised in English tradition, she might have been as great a ruler as England's Elizabeth I. For Elizabeth of Russia possessed diplomatic skill and good judgment. She had charm and much of the fire of her father, Peter the Great.

But during the course of her twenty-one-year rule she gave way increasingly to her caprices, her vanities, and the taste for extravagance she had inherited from her servant-girl mother. In an impoverished land she kept fifteen thousand dresses in her closets.

Fleeing the burdens imposed by her wastefulness, peasants and serfs ran off to Siberia, to the Caucasus, to Poland. Those who did not flee rebelled repeatedly. Elizabeth's solution, the same solution that her predecessors and her successors generally arrived at, was to tighten the restrictions on the common people and lessen the responsibilities of the nobility in order to keep its support. Autocracy has no other choice if it is to remain autocracy. Thus Elizabeth, who had the talent and the opportunity to take Russia another step toward greatness, failed. But she did one thing her father had not succeeded in doing: she passed on the crown to a ruler worthy of Russia's immensity—Catherine the Great.

Her name was not rightly Catherine. It was Sophia Augusta Frederica: "Fike" to her family. She was not Russian, but German. She was not of the Russian Orthodox faith, but Protestant. Her bookish, middle-aged father was the prince of the tiny German state of Anhalt-Zerbst. But the family was impoverished; and, even worse for a girl, Catherine was no beauty. "I do not know if I was actually ugly as a child," she wrote later in her fascinating memoirs, "but I know that I was so often told that I was and that because of this I should try to acquire wit and other merits that until the age of fourteen or fifteen I was convinced that I was a regular ugly duckling and tried much more to acquire these other virtues than rely upon my face."

On New Year's Day, 1744, dinner at the home of the Prince of Anhalt-Zerbst, Fike's father, was interrupted by the arrival of a courier bearing letters. Quick-eyed Fike recognized by the handwriting that some of them came from the Empress Elizabeth's court, and she glimpsed the words "with the Princess, her elder daughter." Her parents quickly went into the next room to talk behind closed doors. But Fike immediately guessed that she and her mother were being invited to Russia so that Elizabeth could determine whether Fike would make a suitable bride for the next emperor. It was a shrewd guess, since Fike had no way of knowing that Prussia's Frederick the Great, anxious to renew Prussia's influence in Russia, had quietly recommended her to Elizabeth.

Fike's parents were reluctant. To them, life in backward Russia was a fate worse than death. But Fike, who soon startled her parents by announcing that she knew all about the invitation, argued that the whole course of her life was at stake. The invitation had to be accepted.

Thus, accompanied by her mother and carrying three dresses sent by Elizabeth so that she would have something to wear at court, Fike made the painful six weeks'

Hunting in Russia, KUTEPOV, 1896–1911

Empress Anne ruled before Elizabeth. Here she indulges in her favorite sport, shooting in a park.

Catherine had the innate ability to be everything her husband was not: a sensitive but strong ruler in Russia and a diplomat abroad (in the painting above by Cornelius Hoier she is seen negotiating with Sweden's King Gustav III).

journey by coach and sleigh to Russia. Upon arriving in Moscow, she soon charmed Elizabeth.

Fike already knew the boy she was to marry. He was a second cousin, the son of Elizabeth's late sister, Anne, Duchess of Holstein. Fike had met him when he was a handsome, likeable lad of eleven, a devout Protestant named Charles Peter Ulrich who was in line to become king of Sweden. Now he was seventeen and Grand Duke Peter of Russia. To make him her heir, Elizabeth had summoned him from his home in Holstein, changed his name, forced him to convert to the Orthodox faith, and signed away his claim to Sweden's throne. Peter detested everything she had done. He loved Holstein and he hated Russia. He despised all things Russian so much that he quarreled bitterly with Elizabeth whenever she ordered him to take a much-needed Russian steam bath. In his resentment he had become an ugly, deceitful, and obstinate boy who refused to grow up. He was completely unready for marriage.

But Elizabeth insisted. And Fike was ready to do anything and marry anybody for a chance to become an empress. She changed her name to Catherine because the name Sophia reminded Russians of Peter the Great's hairy-faced half-sister. She changed her religion with enthusiasm, though she had been a Protestant. She hopped out of bed in the middle of the night, barefoot and in a nightgown, to study Russian (and barely survived the pleurisy she developed as a result). She was as determined to be Russian as young Peter was determined not to be.

The marriage was a disaster. In its early years Peter loaded the bed with dolls and toy soldiers and played with them until he fell asleep. In its later years he offered affection to every woman in the court except his wife. Lonely, ignored or insulted by her husband, often mistreated by the capricious Empress Elizabeth, Catherine plunged into study of the liberal French philosophers whose ideas were transforming the world. She wrote books and plays. She hunted like a man, in the cold and the wet. She rode a horse as though she were determined to break her neck, and she so impressed her riding master that he kissed her boots. She involved herself in love affairs with handsome courtiers and guardsmen and bore a son, Paul, whom Peter grudgingly accepted as his own. But Catherine could not even enjoy motherhood, for Elizabeth took the child away from her, and Catherine rarely saw the boy. For seventeen years she was miserable; once she attempted to

Peter III loved toy soldiers. A rat once spoiled his line-up, so he court-martialed and hanged it.

When Catherine became empress, she brought style, dignity, and a sense of grandeur to Russia. She was a consummate showman, but not to the extent imagined by this painter. He portrayed her visit to the Crimea as being heralded by angels and witnessed by Peter the Great from a heavenly cloud.

kill herself, but the Russian knife was so dull that it failed to pierce her corset.

Then Elizabeth died.

Peter, now thirty-five years old, clowned throughout the long, pomp-filled funeral procession, and even courtiers who shared his relief had to blush for him. But Catherine, who had little reason herself to grieve, shrewdly went into deep mourning.

Six months of Peter as emperor were too much even for a Russia well used to incompetent autocrats. Some of Peter's decrees showed a foolishness bordering on insanity: among the first was one permitting nobles to hunt in the streets of St. Petersburg.

Other decrees had more serious implications. Always a worshiper of Frederick the Great, Peter hastily signed a treaty which not only ended the long war between Russia and Prussia but committed Russian soldiers to fight former allies on Frederick's behalf. Prouder of being the Duke of Holstein than of being ruler of the world's most expansive empire, Peter filled Russia's government with arrogant Holsteiners, ordered a splendid Russian Guard regiment replaced with Holstein troops, and prepared to embroil his bankrupt country in a new war against Denmark to win a few square miles of soil for Holstein.

To Russian patriots the young Emperor had become insufferable. In the streets and in the barracks men muttered about ridding the country of him.

To Catherine, Peter had become a real danger as well as an unfaithful, insulting husband. In a drunken fury he had ordered her arrest and only with difficulty had been talked out of his intentions.

For weeks Catherine's few close friends had been pressing her to seize the throne. She hesitated. It was a throne to which she had no right. Furthermore, Peter, whatever his faults, was her husband. But while she hesitated, the friends conspired. The plans were ready.

On the night of June 27, 1762, one of those friends, a Lieutenant Passek, was arrested. Passek had drunk too much and a secret agent of Peter's had heard him utter dangerous words. Time was racing. Under torture Passek might reveal everything.

At six o'clock next morning Captain Alexei Orlov of the Preobrazhensky Regiment slipped into Catherine's bedroom in a country palace nineteen miles from St. Petersburg. Alexei was the brother of Catherine's sweetheart, Gregory Orlov. He touched her shoulder gently. "You must get up,'' he said as she waked. Catherine asked what had happened, and Orlov replied, "Passek has been arrested."

With Orlov's shouts and the driver's whip spurring on the tired horses which had traversed the road once that night, Catherine raced toward St. Petersburg. A few miles from the city Gregory Orlov and a fellow conspirator met them. Catherine changed to their carriage with its fresher horses and sped on again, dust from the road graying her black dress. At the barracks of the Ismailovsky Regiment on the city's outskirts, drums waked a handful of troops who straggled out half clad. "I beseech your protection," said Catherine. "The Emperor has ordered my arrest; he plans to kill me and my son."

Sources for Russian Iconography, ROVINSKI. 1884 - 90

CONSTANTINOPLE

WARSAW

QUEEN CATHERINE'S DREAM,

Foreign observers of Catherine's rise were fearful of her ambitions. This British cartoon shows the Empress being tempted by a devil who is holding out to her the capital cities of Warsaw and Constantinople. Toward the end of her reign she did seize much of Poland, but Turkey eluded her grasp.

102

Disheveled, flushed with excitement in the dawnlight, Catherine epitomized beauty in distress. And she was the empress. The soldiers cheered. "Long live our little mother Catherine!" A priest emerged with a crucifix: the Orlovs had had him ready. The soldiers ceased kissing the hem of Catherine's skirt and fell silent while the priest prayed briefly. When he had finished, the soldiers cheered again, this time deliriously. Catherine had been proclaimed sole ruler of Russia. But only by a country priest and a few guardsmen. Would the rest of Russia accept her? She hurried on to the quarters of the Semionovsky Regiment, with the excited Ismailovsky Guard following her carriage in disorder.

On her way to the throne, and after being crowned, Catherine was aided by her lovers. Gregory Potemkin (above), one of Catherine's prime ministers, had charming but fake villages put up along the route of her Crimean trip to make her think the peasants were prospering (left).

103

Horsemen had awakened the Semionovsky Guard. Before Catherine reached their barracks they came running out to meet her, uniforms unbuttoned but weapons gleaming. Again the cry went up, "Long live our little mother Catherine." The Semionovsky Guard joined the procession.

But danger lay ahead. The Preobrazhensky Regiment hesitated. Among its officers was one close to Peter. Stirringly he reminded the troops of their duty to the Emperor. Persuaded, the Preobrazhensky Regiment marched out to crush the rebellion. The two columns came face to face. Then Prince Menshikov, a Preobrazhensky officer, cried, "Long live our little mother Catherine, Empress of Russia!" The Preobrazhenskys took up the cheer. The crisis was over.

Excited, delighted citizens poured into the streets. Church bells pealed. With robed priests preceding her carriage and thousands of soldiers and civilians following it, Catherine rode to the already jammed Kazan Cathedral to be sworn as Empress and Autocrat of all the Russias, and then she proceeded to the Winter Palace. Only four hours had passed since Captain Orlov had waked her, alone and in fear, nineteen miles away.

Two tragedies clouded Catherine's reign from the beginning. The first involved the fate of her husband. He had been away carousing at a distant palace, and when he learned of his wife's *coup*, he tried resistance, he tried flight, and then he crumbled, begging only her forgiveness and her permission to return to his beloved Holstein. Catherine dared not let him go, for he would be a threat as long as he lived. So she shipped him off to a country house under guard of the Orlovs. There he drank and gamed with them

In 1773 a fierce uprising against Catherine was led by a clever Cossack named Emelian Pugachev, who pretended to be the deposed Peter III. Peasants flocked to join him; workers brought him cannons (above). But he was caught, caged (left), and executed on a scaffold in Moscow's Red Square.

until one day Catherine received a dreadful letter. Peter, it said, had died in a brawl. Catherine never denied the whispers that she had ordered Peter killed, but her conscience was clear. The Orlovs, who had strangled Peter, had not acted on her instructions.

The second tragedy involved Ivan VI, from whom Elizabeth had snatched the throne more than two decades earlier when he was an infant. The unfortunate lad had grown up in solitary confinement, unschooled, barely able to talk because no one ever talked to him. His ignorant guards did not even know who he was. A disgruntled infantry officer with dreams of glory hatched a plot to rescue Ivan and place him on the throne. With a handful of men the misguided officer attacked the fortress where Ivan was imprisoned. A brutal soldier, carrying out orders given long before, promptly stabbed Ivan through the heart to prevent his liberation. Ivan VI, Emperor of Russia when he was too young to know it, died without ever having seen the sky.

But for most Russians the sky seemed to brighten after Catherine's accession. Influenced by her wide reading of the works of enlightened Europeans and by her correspondence with such men as Voltaire, she drew up an Instruction for a legislative commission which she summoned. It was admittedly borrowed from the Frenchman Montesquieu's *The Spirit of the Law* and from the Italian Beccaria's *Crimes and Punishments* and it was a radical document for the times. It said men were equal before the law. It said freedom was the right to do anything not forbidden by law. It said law existed to prevent crime rather than to punish it. It said no country should be divided into a few large estates. It said that serfdom should be limited. It proposed the abolition of torture, the establishment of a jury system with peasants sitting among the judges, and the extension of education.

But nothing came of Catherine's good intentions. In the Russia of the time nothing could have come of them, for Catherine needed the nobility's support to retain her throne, and the nobility would permit no limitations of its privileges. So under Catherine, as under her predecessors, the rich grew richer and the poor grew poorer to the point once again of civil war. When a former Don Cossack named Emelian Pugachev, another of Russia's many pretenders, announced that he was Peter III and promised to free the serfs, he won thousands of followers among Cossacks and peasants, and among Bashkirs, Kal-

Catherine was still a handsome woman in her old age (above). Among her passions was a love for classical architecture; the rebuilding of her palace near St. Petersburg (below) was carried out in the proper international style of the eighteenth century.

mucks, Kirghiz, Tatars, and Finns, who had been absorbed by Russia's expansion. Before Pugachev was hunted down and executed, hundreds of manor houses had been burned to the ground, thousands of landowners, merchants, and priests had been tortured and murdered. Frightened by the Pugachev rebellion and confirmed in her fears by the French Revolution's Reign of Terror, Catherine the Great became another tyrant.

But if Catherine failed in her domestic policies, she triumphed magnificently in her foreign policies, and these were her own. Her methods were the methods of the time, and utterly immoral by our standards, but she used them brilliantly. Shamelessly she refused to admit the success of the French Revolution or the humanity of its ideals; she would not let the tri-colored French flag be flown in a Russian harbor. Shamelessly she participated in the partition of Poland, over which she installed one of her former favorites as king. Shamelessly she grabbed territories to which Russia had only fragile claims going back to the era of Kievan Rus; thereby she earned for herself (many times over) the title she bore—Empress and Autocrat of all the Russias.

During Catherine's reign, Russia's borders were pushed farther east and west, almost to its present size except for areas bordering China.

When she died on November 16, 1796, after thirty-four years of rule, Sophia Augusta Frederica of Anhalt-Zerbst, who had become Catherine the Great of Russia, had made Russia an even mightier European power than Peter had dreamed of making it.

*A visitor to Moscow in 1800 would immediately note the city's sharp con-
trasts: wooden huts and gilded spires; peasants, guardsmen, and philosophers.*

THE MYSTERY OF ALEXANDER

Czar after czar—even Ivan the Terrible—had come to the throne determined to gain mass support by easing the plight of the peasants. And czar after czar, faced with losing the support of the nobility if he did help the serfs, had changed his mind. The serf was worse off than before.

Russia had not always been a land of serfs. In the great days of Kiev and Novgorod most men had been free. Only prisoners of war and bankrupts had become serfs, and even they might buy their liberty. But over the centuries the czars had extended their own landholdings and had bestowed great estates, along with the people who dwelt on them, upon supporters who helped them attain or retain the throne. These lands had to be tilled or timber had to be cut, but free peasants were not dependable tillers and lumberers: they were forever moving to rival estates that offered better pay, or heading east to pioneer far from regions of war and famine. Without workers the landowning nobility would collapse; without the nobility the czars feared the throne would collapse. So little by little, decree by decree, the free peasants had lost their freedom of movement, and then every other freedom.

Alexander I, grandson of Catherine the Great, appeared to be of a different breed from his predecessors. When he came to the throne in 1801, he appeared willing and able to do something about the lot of the serfs.

As handsome as his father (Catherine's son, Emperor Paul) had been ugly, he charmed the court ladies. He was also as keen of intellect as his father had been muddled. Ascending the throne at twenty-four, he envisioned himself as a Western-style king, and he spoke bitterly of "the state of barbarism in which the country has been left by the traffic in men."

Alexander promptly abolished the secret police, pardoned thousands of political prisoners and exiles, and forbade the use of torture in the questioning of suspects. He reopened the doors that Catherine and Paul had slammed

OVERLEAF: *This colorful painting of the French army assault on Smolensk shows the city being set afire, Scythian style, by the retreating Russians.*
MUSEE DE L'ARMEE

shut against liberal foreign ideas. Students could again travel abroad. Foreigners and foreign books could again enter the country; closed publishing houses could print the books with which a few brilliant minds were initiating a great upsurge of Russian literature and culture.

The right to own land, a right previously restricted to the nobility, was granted to all classes of society except serfs. Even a state peasant (one of the fourteen million workers on government land) might become a proprietor. The sale of serfs was limited, and the practice of giving state peasants to nobles as serfs was abandoned.

Within eight years of his coronation, Alexander empowered Michael Speransky, the brilliant son of a village priest, to draft a constitution. He produced a remarkably wise document designed to establish representative government—with even some representation from the peasant class.

It was a time of historic suspense. Could and would Alexander make Russia free despite the nobility?

The Napoleonic wars delayed the answer. Although at first neither Alexander nor Napoleon wanted to fight each other, Alexander came to believe that he had a divine mission to oppose "the oppressor of Europe and the disturber of the world's peace."

The task that he set himself was a huge one, beset by discouragements. When Alexander leagued Russia with England, Sweden, and Austria in 1805 to free Northern Germany, Holland, Switzerland, and Italy from Napoleon, a French army trounced ninety thousand Russians and Austrians at Austerlitz in Moravia (now Czechoslovakia). Alexander wept. When Napoleon secretly plotted to carve up France's own ally, Prussia, Alexander went to Prussia's defense. Again the French defeated the Russians, this time at Friedland in East Prussia. Without effective allies, his treasury bare, his army demoralized after a brave fight, and his country restive, Alexander had to adopt a more conciliatory policy. And thus it was that the two men, Alexander and Napoleon, met on a raft on the Niemen River on June 25, 1807, to swear eternal friendship, as Adolf Hitler and Joseph Stalin pledged eternal friendship almost a century and a half later. Together, Napoleon and Alexander would bring peace to the world by conquering it.

The friendship could not endure. Neither man fulfilled the obligations that the other imposed. Mutual suspicions festered. Convinced finally that he could be master of Europe only if he overcame Russia, Napoleon struck, fought his way to Moscow, and retreated disastrously.

Sources for Russian Iconography, ROVINSKI, 1884–90

Catherine's son Paul was eccentric, ugly, and widely hated, as is reflected by this caricature. Paul was strangled by officers in 1801.

SOVFOTO

European Russia, KENNAN, 1936

Peasants had no more rights than farm animals in nineteenth-century Russia; they could be traded for dogs (above). Increasing restrictions had reduced the peasant class, some thirty million Russians, to the status of serfs, half of whom were owned by the czarist state itself. At left is a photograph of a group of peasants at a country fair.

113

Russian Historical Pictures, ORLOV, 1911

Sources for Russian Iconography, ROVINSKI, 1884–

Before the conflict, Napoleon and Alexander embraced on a raft in the Niemen River (left). Their officers viewed the meeting skeptically.

When the tide of battle turned in Alexander's favor, a British cartoonist drew the Russian bear hugging a scrawny Napoleon (below left).

Despite a disgraceful retreat from the French at Smolensk, General Barclay de Tolly was able to redeem himself and later win a promotion.

It was Alexander's turn now. Inspired by a sense of divine mission, he rallied his own armies and a coalition of Europe's powers, won a series of military victories, marched triumphantly into Paris on March 31, 1814, deposed Napoleon, and summoned the Congress of Vienna. That was Alexander's most brilliant moment—and one of Russia's greatest world triumphs. Out of the congress, which met in 1815, came the Holy Alliance, which pledged its members "to take as their sole guide . . . the precepts of religion, namely the rules of justice, Christian charity, and peace . . . They will consider themselves as members of one and the same Christian nation." Almost every Christian monarch in Europe joined. Alexander had achieved his ideal and could go back to reforming Russia in peace.

Again, it was a time of opportunity. Liberal ideas flourished among young, educated noblemen. Secret societies discussed plans for a new Russia in which even serfs would be free. Journalists wrote as they pleased, poets and dramatists produced works of beauty.

But, as had happened before in Russia and as would happen again, the promise was not fulfilled. In the twenty-four years of Alexander's reign, only forty-seven thousand out of the twenty million serfs gained freedom. Few state peasants became landowners. The constitution that Michael Speransky had drawn up moldered in a pigeonhole. Why?

The answers lie in the nature of Russia, in the nature of Alexander, in the nature of autocracy.

Of serfdom Alexander once said: "If [our] civilization were more advanced, I would abolish this slavery if it cost me my head." But Russia's civilization was not more advanced despite the young nobles, despite the poets and the dramatists. Had Alexander ended serfdom by decree

After Alexander's death, the Decembrists (wearing slouch hats in the melodramatic sketch at right) tried to stage the first popular revolution in the history of Russia.

and deprived the aristocracy of its field hands and house servants, he would indeed have lost his head.

And although Alexander was sincere in his intention to establish constitutional government, he was a complex man beneath his outward charm, and no one ever knew what he really was thinking. A liberal by education, he was an autocrat by heredity, and the heredity gradually submerged the liberal. "You always want to instruct me," he once chided one of his ministers. "I am the autocratic emperor and I will do this . . ." As an autocrat he could not quite trust the people he wanted to lead into freedom.

Alexander thus ceased to be the hope of his country, and now men even whispered of revolution, for the winds of liberty were still blowing in the world. Burdened by his problems, disappointed at his failure to solve them, Alexander began to talk of abdicating when he was fifty. He was forty-eight when he was stricken with fever, and on December 1, 1825, it was announced that he had died in Taganrog in the Crimea.

All his life Alexander had been something of a mystery. The mystery did not end with his death. A hermit named Fedor Kuzmich appeared who may have been Alexander

himself. The legend evolved that this recluse, who lived until 1864 and who was always accorded unexplained deference by succeeding czars, really was Alexander I finishing his days as a holy man. But, legend or not, Alexander's coffin was empty when it was opened in the nineteen-twenties.

Alexander's death or disappearance left Russia momentarily in a curious mix-up—without a czar who wanted to rule. And in that moment dawned the Age of Revolution, which ended with the Communist seizure of power a century later.

The mix-up developed because Alexander's wife was childless. Alexander's brother Constantine was next in line for the throne. But Constantine, happily married to a Pole and living comfortably in Warsaw, the capital of Russian-ruled Poland, did not want to be czar. Years earlier he had signed away his rights. At the news that Alexander had died, Constantine ordered the Polish troops whom he commanded to swear loyalty to his younger brother, Nicholas. But Alexander, aware that Nicholas was as much disliked as Constantine was liked, had never told the Russian people that Constantine had refused the crown. Nicholas, smart enough to realize his own unpopularity, dared not proclaim himself czar, and in St. Petersburg he ordered his troops to swear allegiance to Constantine. For almost three weeks couriers raced back and forth between Warsaw and St. Petersburg. Constantine would not take the trouble to go to St. Petersburg to abdicate publicly, and Nicholas feared that nobody would believe a letter.

The confusion provided the opportunity for which a small band of well-born, intelligent young men—princes, army officers, economists—had long been preparing.

Russia's countless serf rebellions, born of anger and despair, had lacked purpose other than desperate, vengeful destruction. Russia's many palace revolutions had been designed only to replace one czar with another. The revolution that these young men and their secret associates had in mind would be the first in Russia's history that was motivated by ideals and by a program for progress—though just what the program would be they were not sure.

On December 26, 1825, after they had informed army friends all over Russia of their plans and had won promises of support, the revolutionary Guard officers among the plotters massed several thousand of their troops before the Council of State building in St. Petersburg's Senate Square. At the officers' urging, the troops shouted, "Con-

stantine and Constitution! Constantine and Constitution!"
The soldiers had been told that Nicholas was trying to cheat
Constantine of the throne. Many of them, unlettered serfs
drafted from nobles' estates, thought "Constitution" was
the name of Constantine's wife. Troops loyal to Nicholas
poured into nearby streets. Neither side knew quite what
to do. For hours the two forces faced each other, swinging
their arms and stamping in the bitter cold. Occasionally
civilians threw stones at Nicholas' soldiers, occasionally
somebody fired a few shots and a few men fell dead. Nicholas
sent Count Miloradovich, Governor-General of St. Petersburg, to talk to the mutineers, and a rattled lieutenant
fatally wounded him.

Darkness approached: if night came before the rebels
had been dispersed, Nicholas feared that real fighting
and perhaps civil war would follow. So Nicholas sent
cavalry against the rebels. The rebels stood their ground.
Then he brought up cannon. At the third volley, the in-
surgents fled. About seventy bodies, civilians among them,
lay in the square. The risings scheduled elsewhere never
took place. The revolution was over.

Suave and charming, cloaked in the manner of a kind
father reasoning with a disobedient child, Nicholas personally questioned the conspirators and elicited full con-
fessions, which Russians so often seem eager to make when
caught defying authority. In the months-long investiga-
tions that followed, some 600 persons were arrested and
121 held for trial. Michael Speransky, the brilliant liberal
who had drawn up a constitution for Alexander, was
among the judges who sentenced 5 of the plotters to be
quartered, 31 to be beheaded, and the rest to suffer solitary
confinement in fortresses or forced labor in Siberia's
coal mines.

All Russia was shocked. Execution had gone out of
style in Empress Elizabeth's day. And although Nicholas
commuted the death sentences of all but five conspirators,
Russians have never forgotten the Decembrist martyrs,
as these doomed revolutionaries were called. Their revolution was inept and vague, but its effects on the Russian
people were great. The sparks of revolution that would
burst into the flaming holocaust of 1917 were beginning to
crackle across the land.

To the later czars, Alexander I (at left) bequeathed his blue eyes and his
fine physique. But he also passed along his inability to modernize Russia.

VIII

REVOLUTION!

COURTESY OF THE OLD PRINT SHOP, NEW YORK

Alexander II freed Russia's serfs but it was too late to save Russia.

It was March 3, 1861. All over Russia criers hurried into muddy village squares to intone the news. And by the millions the serfs knelt in thanksgiving. One day before Abraham Lincoln's inauguration in America, Nicholas' son, Alexander II, abolished serfdom. He had accomplished the impossible because it had become impossible to do anything else. Thirty years of repression by Nicholas I had failed to crush the unrest revealed by the Decembrist revolt and had left the country impoverished, backward, corrupt, and filled with fear of a serf uprising.

Russia's shortcomings had also helped to defeat her in the Crimean War in which Nicholas had foolishly embroiled the country. That defeat made Alexander and thousands of other Russians realize that Russia would cease to count as a power in Europe unless she redesigned and rebuilt her social and economic structure.

Serfdom was the base of the structure, and Alexander destroyed it. It was a moment of tremendous promise, and Alexander seemed to be fulfilling the promise when he instituted other reforms. But he was creating new problems for himself. Russians had tasted freedom, and appetite grows with tasting. The emancipation of the serfs had transformed most peasants into tenant farmers with too little land and had tied the rest to collective farms. The former serfs now clamored for a second emancipation that would give them more land and other freedoms. The nobles demanded a constitution and a legislature. Alexander called a halt. There would be no second emancipation, no free speech, no legislature. To some radical students, violent revolution, not reform, now became Russia's only hope.

On April 16, 1866, as Alexander entered a carriage in

Climax of the Russian Revolution of 1917 was the seizure of the Winter Palace in St. Petersburg by a Bolshevik-led mob of soldiers and sailors.

121

St. Petersburg, a student named Dmitry Karakozov fired his pistol at him. The shot missed. But it inspired new repressions and set off a struggle between revolutionaries and czars that lasted to 1917. Students barred from universities for radical ideas formed secret cells to conspire for a democratic regime or a socialist state; a few joined a murderous movement called nihilism, or nothingism, which preached "terrible, total, universal, and merciless destruction of society" to bring about "the entire emancipation and happiness of the people." Secret presses poured out propaganda; secret workshops produced forged passports. Revolutionaries infiltrated the government. Even the frail and beautiful Sophie Perovskaya, daughter of the governor-general of St. Petersburg, was a Nihilist. Plots brought reprisals, reprisals brought new plots. A mine was laid in front of Alexander's train. He escaped. A revolutionary carpenter smuggled dynamite into the Winter

Harper's Weekly

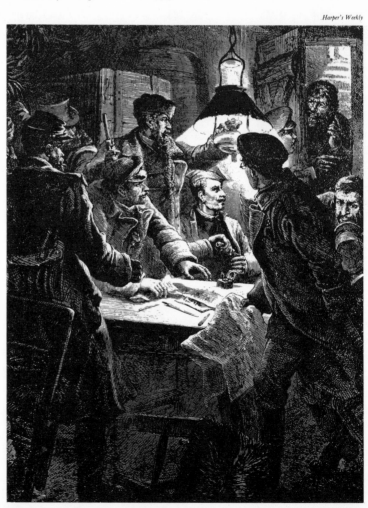

The most wild-eyed revolutionaries in the time of Alexander II were Nihilists. Here a group of them is warned that police are coming.

The assassination of Alexander II was a dramatic forecast of future violence. This scene haunted the two czars who followed Alexander.

Palace and set it off as Alexander awaited a dinner guest. The blast killed or wounded forty Finnish guards, but Alexander escaped again.

The revolutionary spirit spread. Alexander's advisers urged him to establish a legislature to win back popular support. He agreed, and on March 13, 1881, he signed the document. Russia was taking a great step toward democracy.

But it was too late. That same day Alexander reviewed some troops, dined with an aunt, and went out in his carriage. A Nihilist threw a bomb. It wounded some of Alexander's Cossack guards, and he stepped down to help them. He gently reproved the would-be assassin, whom the police had seized, and thanked God for his own escape. "It is too early to thank God," cried a young man nearby as he threw a second bomb. Alexander fell, his body shattered. "Home to the palace to die," he commanded.

Among the five conspirators who died on the gallows for the killing was Sophie Perovskaya.

A wise new czar might have ended the threat of revolution then and there. Alexander II's assassination had shocked Russians into renewed loyalty to the crown. And Alexander had left behind him a different land from the one he had inherited. Great books were being written, and great music was being composed (see page 130). Great scientists were at work: by 1874 a student named A. Ladygin had demonstrated that electricity could be used for illumination. Railroads were being built—ten thousand miles of them during the decade from 1866 to 1876—and railroads expanded industry, which provided jobs for former serfs. Some serfs entered industry and improved their lot. Russia was still far behind the West, still a difficult and unhappy land for most Russians. Nevertheless, Russia was progressing enough to warrant the hope that reform might yet outpace revolution.

But Alexander III disliked reform as much as revolution. Undoing almost everything his father had done, though he could not reestablish serfdom, he antagonized every class of Russian—and terrorism flared anew. Among the new terrorists was a young man named Alexander Ulyanov, son of a government school inspector who had been ennobled. Trapped in an 1887 plot against Alexander's life, Ulyanov died on the gallows. His seventeen-year-old brother, swearing vengeance, became a revolutionary too, and like all revolutionaries he took an assumed name, Lenin.

When Alexander III died on November 1, 1894, exhausted by his almost single-handed efforts to maintain autocracy, the race between reform and revolution was quickening. But its result was far from decided.

Alexander's son, Nicholas II, was hardly the man even to know that the race was being run. He was handsome, charming, gentle to the point of weakness, religious to the point of mysticism. His marriage to the beautiful Princess Alix of Hesse-Darmstadt, the equally religious and mystical granddaughter of England's Queen Victoria, was a love

For centuries the rulers of czarist Russia were crowned amid the gilded frescoes of the Kremlin's Ouspensky Cathedral (right). The ominous events of Nicholas II's coronation gave him the nickname Bloody Nicholas.

match. But the young rulers were autocrats—and Nicholas announced at the start that nothing would change.

The reign began with two evil omens. At the coronation, a chain symbolizing the Russian empire fell from Nicholas' breast. At the festivities after the coronation, clumsy official arrangements produced a stampede among thousands of persons gathered in a field outside Moscow to receive gifts; between one thousand and three thousand were crushed to death. The fallen chain haunted Nicholas with the expectation of doom, and his attendance at the French ambassador's ball the night of the tragedy in the field cost him much of the affection his people had already bestowed on him. But the first years of his reign were relatively peaceful, though now and again an assassin's shot felled an official, or the police had to crush a strike. In any case, Nicholas was chiefly concerned with his family.

His beloved but domineering wife, rechristened Alexandra, bore four daughters. Both wanted a son; they were delighted when a boy arrived on July 30, 1904. But their joy was short-lived. The child suffered from the inherited ailment of his mother's House of Hesse, the disease called hemophilia, in which the blood fails to clot and a minor cut may prove fatal.

Nicholas and Alexandra prayed daily for a miracle. The "miracle" came on November 1, 1905, when they were introduced to Gregory, a wandering, bearded religious pilgrim of giant physique and hypnotic eyes who had the power to halt the little boy's bleeding. It made no difference to Nicholas and Alexandra that Gregory was called Rasputin, which means debauched, and that he had well earned the nickname. From then on Rasputin dominated Alexandra, as she already dominated her husband.

Meanwhile, beneath Russia's comparatively placid surface there were revolutionary stirrings again. As far back as 1861 a book called *Das Kapital*, laboriously written in London's British Museum by a bearded, expatriated German named Karl Marx, had slipped into Russia because the censor found it too difficult to understand. The book forecast the destruction of capitalism, that is, the private ownership of wealth, and its replacement by socialism, in which all the people jointly would own everything. Because the book was so hard to read it got little attention in Russia at the time. But a young idealist named George Plekhanov, who had read the book, went to Switzerland where in 1883 he organized a few fellow Russian exiles to work for Marxian socialism. A moderate man,

Focus of all Russia's discontent was Nicholas II. Handsome and charming, he had the misfortune to have no minister wise enough and strong enough to help him keep his crown. Instead he leaned on his willful wife. The royal couple is shown here surrounded by their four daughters and one son (second from left). The family was cruelly executed by Communist soldiers in 1918.

The two bearded Germans above wrote the provocative book that soon became the Communists' bible. It was Das Kapital, *which Frederick Engels (on the right) completed after the death of his colleague, Karl Marx. The first Russian translation of* Das Kapital *(right) was published in 1872. It had little appeal for Russian liberals because its ideas against private property did not seem right for a country of entrenched landowners and stubborn peasants.*

КАПИТАЛЪ.

КРИТИКА ПОЛИТИЧЕСКОЙ ЭКОНОМІИ.

СОЧИНЕНІЕ
КАРЛА МАРКСА.

ПЕРЕВОДЪ СЪ НѢМЕЦКАГО.

ТОМЪ ПЕРВЫЙ.

КНИГА I. ПРОЦЕССЪ ПРОИЗВОДСТВА КАПИТАЛА.

С.-ПЕТЕРБУРГЪ.
ИЗДАНІЕ Н. П. ПОЛЯКОВА.
1872

Plekhanov preached moderate methods of putting socialism into practice. His ideas filtered into Russia; by 1895
the young man who called himself Lenin organized a secret
society in St. Petersburg to preach Marxism among factory
workers. The police shipped Lenin to Siberia. But in 1898
several groups similar to Lenin's founded the Russian
Social Democratic Workers party. The police broke up the
party; after his release from prison, Lenin joined Plekhanov
in Switzerland. Master and disciple quickly disagreed.
Plekhanov believed socialism could triumph only after
most Russians had been educated under democracy.
Lenin argued that a small, dedicated band of Marxists
should arouse factory, mine, and shipyard workers to
immediate revolution, and that socialism could be instituted thereafter.

The dispute split the little party. Lenin's followers took
the name Bolshevik, meaning majority, and his opponents

*This famous painting by I. E. Repin shows both the overbearing attitude of
the czar's mounted police and the pageantry of an Orthodox Church procession. A group of cripples hurry to touch the sacred icons and be cured.*

the name Menshevik, meaning minority. The Mensheviks included a young man named Leo Bronstein who called himself Leon Trotsky.

Instead of countering these, and more moderate democratic, non-socialist parties, by reforms, Nicholas and his secret police tried to stamp out the opposition. Police agents infiltrated the revolutionary parties and occasionally rose to leadership in them. One amazing operative named Evno Azef was for years both a police spy and an active terrorist who directed the assassination of one of Nicholas' ministers. His police superiors accepted his explanation that by the murder he had diverted the plotters from an attempt to kill Nicholas.

Labor unions were illegal. But the police actually organized unions and led strikes to distract the workers from revolutionary propaganda.

The police strategy backfired, and the backfire sparked revolution. In 1904 Russia had become involved in a disastrous and unpopular war with Japan; the resulting hunger, the mounting casualty lists, and the disclosures of government corruption had set Russians seething with shame and discontent, just as after the Crimean War. The government would have to change its ways. From a conference of the local *zemstvos*, the only elected groups in the country, came requests for a representative national legislature, freedom of speech and of worship, equality for all, and improved conditions for workers and peasants.

Nicholas scoffed. His response rallied journalists, educators, artists, to support the *zemstvo* proposals. Then on January 22, 1905, came Bloody Sunday.

George Gapon, an Orthodox priest who was a police agent, had been installed as head of the police-organized labor unions. Gapon apparently took seriously the task of bettering the lives of the workers. So on the day that was to become Bloody Sunday, he summoned the workers to

Michael Glinka

Alexander Borodin

Nikolai Rimsky-Korsakov

Russia in the nineteenth century was swarming with assassins and revolutionaries. But it was also alive with great artists. Early in the century Alexander Pushkin wrote poetry that still seems freshly romantic; toward the end of the century Count Leo Tolstoy and Fedor Dostoevsky wrote novels reflecting the social struggles that would eventually lead to the Revolution of 1917. In music, Michael Glinka was the first composer to combine Russian themes with "foreign" European musical forms. And the music of Peter Ilich Tchaikovsky soon became renowned around the world. Others, however, were dedicated to composing peculiarly Russian music; among them, Nikolai Rimsky-Korsakov, Alexander Borodin, and Modest Moussorgsky.

Peter Ilich Tchaikovsky

Modest Moussorgsky

Count Leo Tolstoy

Alexander Pushkin

Fedor Dostoevsky

present their grievances to Nicholas. From all over St. Petersburg orderly processions carrying sacred icons and singing religious and patriotic songs converged on the Winter Palace. Troops which the government had posted to stop them opened fire; hundreds of workers fell dead.

The shots of the troops and the repressive measures that followed unified every opposition force, actual and potential, in the country. Government officials resigned in disgust. Workers, professional men, even school boys, went on strike. A bomb killed Nicholas' uncle, and the assassin, to demonstrate his scorn of the government, did not try to escape or to appeal for mercy. The crew of the battleship *Potemkin* mutinied and spread terror along the coast of the Black Sea. Peasants drove landowners from their estates and embarked on a reign of terror.

The disorders raged for months. A spontaneous general strike paralyzed the country. No railroads ran. No power plants produced electricity; gas and water supplies petered

Before World War I Russia had already been engaged in two disastrous inter-national contests: the Crimean War (best remembered for the famous Charge of the Light Brigade—at left) and the Russo-Japanese War of 1904 in which the Russian fleet (above) showed itself inadequate for modern warfare.

133

THE FINAL SPLENDOR OF THE CZARS

While Russia was humiliated abroad and split with internal strife, the royal family continued to occupy that ancient citadel of the czars, the Kremlin. Decorated with a series of religious and historical murals, the Throne Room (below) of the Terim Palace was typical of the Kremlin's splendor. Other apartments were filled with sumptuous treasures like the enamel tankard and the jeweled Easter egg at right, both of which were made but a few decades before the Russian Revolution.

135

out. No telephones operated. Schools, banks, stores, courts, even government offices, closed. Crowds roamed the cities with red flags, demanding a democratic republic.

In the chaos, a soviet, or council of delegates elected by workers, convened in St. Petersburg. More soviets organized in other cities. Lenin the Bolshevik was abroad. But Trotsky the Menshevik emerged as a kind of prime minister of a workers' parliamentary government.

In that desperate moment, Serge Witte, a former railway stationmaster who had risen to be a count and an adviser to Nicholas, saved the throne. Witte induced Nicholas to sign a historic proclamation: Russia would have an elected legislature and no laws would take effect without its approval. Furthermore, civil liberties were in force for all.

The wildest excitement engulfed Russia. Only the leaders of the revolutionary parties did not rejoice, for the reform, they realized, would end the revolution. It did. Said Trotsky: "The revolution is dead. Long live the revolution!" Yet most people were satisfied by the arrival of representative government.

Thus, in March, 1906, deputies were elected to the new legislature called the Duma in the first national election ever held in Russia. Its complexion was moderate; radicals won only a few seats, extreme conservatives none.

Under new reforms Russia began to surge forward. Peasants, at last permitted to own enough land to make a living, tilled with new vigor. Once scrabbly farms prospered. Cooperatives sprang up to market farm produce, and exports to other lands increased—although Russia's rapidly growing population continued to eat up most of the food produced. Boom times at home and abroad, and the establishment of representative government, inspired confidence in Russia's future; business and industry thrived. Wages rose, illiteracy diminished.

Yet most peasants lived in leaky cottages without chimneys. Industrial workers still earned far less than their fellows in Western Europe. Russia's captive lands, especially Poland and Finland, still chafed under Russian rule, and Jews often were murdered by mobs incited by the police. A handful of revolutionaries still worked underground with advice from leaders abroad, and secret police still infiltrated their ranks. Nevertheless, Russia was emerging into modernity when the First World War exploded.

Patriotism surged throughout the country. Even the socialist parties, with the exception of the absent Lenin's

Russia was ill prepared for World War I. Most of the troops' equipment was as primitive as the sledges seen at left. The government was ailing; neither Nicholas nor anyone else took the legislature, or Duma, seriously. It had once been disbanded by his decree, and its members had met in a wood (below).

small Bolshevik organization, backed the government, and a huge crowd fell to its knees when Nicholas appeared on the balcony of the Winter Palace.

Russia was not ready for a war. Many soldiers went to the front without rifles. The prime minister was a weak old man, the war minister an apathetic fool. An intelligence service colonel was a German spy. The power of Rasputin over Alexandra had become total, and through her he controlled Nicholas.

Although he opposed the war and often predicted defeat, Rasputin ran the government. Day after day letters from Alexandra to Nicholas, who was at the front, passed on Rasputin's advice: more recruits should not be called up, the Duma should not be assembled, Nicholas should advance on the Riga front.

Russian armies inevitably suffered crushing defeats. Then on December 30, 1916, Alexandra wrote to Nicholas despairingly: "Our friend has disappeared. Such utter anguish."

Famine, like the one brought on by World War I, has always threatened the Russians. To relieve the 1891 famine, food from America was sped by troika to the starving peasants.

Only a few young aristocrats knew what had happened to "our friend"—Rasputin. In the hope of saving Russia they had invited him to a midnight supper and plied him with glass after glass of wine mixed with the deadliest of poisons. The poison had no visible effect. Impatient, the conspirators shot Rasputin again and again. At last his mighty body collapsed. The plotters carried Rasputin to an automobile, drove to the Neva River, and pushed the corpse under the ice.

But it was too late to save Russia—if Rasputin's death alone would ever have saved it.

The enemy had overrun most of the west and southwest of the country, and two million refugees had to be cared for. Military demands for supplies overburdened the remaining railways. Food and fuel were running short in the cities. Two million soldiers had been killed, and deserters were spreading defeatist talk. Factory workers, stirred by whispered revolutionary propaganda, were restive. Grand dukes were considering the ouster of Nicholas and his replacement by his son.

On March 8, 1917, the long lines in front of the capital's bakeries became unruly: the people knew there was flour in the city but that it was not being properly distributed, and they clamored for bread. There were scuffles with police. The next day, strikes broke out all over the capital, which had been renamed Petrograd because St. Petersburg sounded German. "Some disorders occurred today," the British ambassador cabled the Foreign Office in London, "but nothing serious."

On March 10 Nicholas ordered troops to fire if the disorder continued. On March 11 czarist soldiers did fire on paraders carrying banners and killed or wounded at least eighty persons.

That night the soldiers talked over what had to be done. They decided they would not obey any more commands to shoot; they had been peasants and workers themselves before they became soldiers. Next morning, March 12, thousands of soldiers comprising virtually all of the 190,000-man Petrograd garrison poured out of their barracks to join the demonstrators.

Together, troops and civilians broke into the arsenal, distributed guns, attacked prisons and freed prisoners, set ablaze headquarters of the secret police, trampled policemen.

It was a spontaneous, leaderless revolution. No political party had sparked it. The total of all the people in Russia

Lustful, illiterate, the evil monk Rasputin used mysticism to dominate the Empress—and became the power behind the czarist regime.

who hoped that some day in the distant future Russia would be socialist was a small minority. Lenin's Bolsheviks were a tiny segment of that minority, and Lenin himself was in Switzerland where he had been waiting out the war. Trotsky was in New York. Joseph Stalin and other future communist leaders were in Siberia, and hardly anyone in Russia had even heard of these men who were soon to become world-famous.

Soldiers, workers, peasants, intellectuals, all had been ready for revolution. But the revolution had not overthrown autocracy. It had given it a push, and autocracy was collapsing.

Someone, some group, had to assume leadership. On the afternoon of March 12 the Duma convened. In the evening it received a telegram from Grand Duke Cyril, a member of the royal family, and from officers of the Preobrazhensky Regiment asking it to take power. Simultaneously, in the same palace where the Duma was meeting, hastily elected delegates from factories and barracks met to organize a soviet, or council. Among the delegates were a few Bolsheviks; most delegates were moderate Socialist Revolutionaries and Mensheviks.

For two days Duma and soviet, barely beyond earshot of each other, debated what to do.

On the fourteenth the Duma voted to set up a Provisional government headed by Prince George Lvov, chairman of the association of *zemstvos*. There was one socialist minister in the new government, Alexander Kerensky, a lawyer.

That same day the soviet prepared its own Order Number One, instructing troops to obey only orders of the soviet. In that order lay the danger of conflict between Duma and soviet. The Duma theoretically represented all the people. The soviet claimed to represent workers and soldiers. Which would win?

On the fifteenth the soviet agreed to support the Duma's Provisional government if free elections were held soon. The new government assented. But the soviet sent out its Order Number One anyway, and thenceforth neither the revolutionary officers nor the new government really controlled the army.

Alexander Kerensky

Leon Trotsky

Trumpeting "Peace, Bread, and Freedom," Bolshevik leaders came out of exile to make the 1917 uprising a Bolshevik revolution. The Provisional government of Alexander Kerensky gave way to a soviet regime under Lenin, at left haranguing a crowd. Trotsky was named commissar for foreign affairs.

141

Meanwhile, Nicholas, hurrying back from the front by train to be with his family in the crisis, found the tracks blocked by revolutionaries. His generals advised him to abdicate, and most pledged their own support to the new government.

Shortly before midnight in his railway car at Pskov, in the presence of two delegates from the Duma, Nicholas II composed his resignation. He ended the document with the words "May the Lord God keep Russia".

It was too late for him to bestow the throne on another. The Duma and the soviet wanted no more Romanovs. Czardom in Russia, which had had its beginnings with the House of Rurik a thousand years before, was ended.

An almost impossible task faced Nicholas' successors, led by Prince Lvov and Kerensky. The economy was in a state of collapse, the army clamored to go home, the conquered Poles and Finns demanded immediate independence, and the people wanted peace.

But unless Russia continued to fight, the Germans would conquer the whole country. The revolution of March, 1917, would have been in vain.

The government decided to battle on, and Kerensky, its real chief, toured the front to rally weary soldiers. Whether or not he would have succeeded, had it not been for a shrewd German *coup*, is endlessly debatable.

The Germans knew little of Lenin except that from Switzerland he had been urging socialists in all countries to stop fighting. Perhaps, they reasoned, it would be worthwhile to send him back to Russia to make trouble. Aboard a sealed railway car that had been granted safe conduct through Germany, Lenin and a handful of fellow Bolsheviks arrived in Petrograd on April 16. Stalin, freed from Siberia by the revolution, was already there. Trotsky, who had come around to Lenin's way of thinking, was on his way from America. They had few followers, but they were tireless zealots with the gifts of persuasiveness and the ability to organize. Their slogan was "Peace, Bread, and Freedom!" Their goal, to the surprise of most Russian socialists, was immediate socialism, to be achieved by a second revolution. The Provisional government stood in the way of the second revolution they proclaimed. Therefore, "All power to the soviets!"

"Peace" was an alluring word to the soldiery. "Bread" won the peasantry. "Freedom" appealed to the industrial workers of the cities and to the national minorities. The Provisional government knew that peace, bread, and free-

dom could come only with victory on the battlefields, and Kerensky managed by superhuman effort to organize a military offensive against the Austrians in July. The first assaults breached the enemy lines and put the Austrian army to flight. But the loyal Russian troops who achieved the triumph got no support from reserves seduced by the vision of peace, bread, and freedom. The reserves quit the fight; the victory was in vain. Worse, men of the Petrograd garrison attempted to overthrow the government, and

The final stroke of the revolution was preceded by more than a year of bitter fighting. In this painting czarist horsemen bear down on rebels who have put up a barricade on Moscow's Gorbatov Bridge.

Sailors from the port of Kronstadt, firing the guns of a commandeered tank (top right), blasted their way through the streets of Petrograd on July 13, 1917, as part of a Bolshevik protest against the Provisional government.

cavalry had to be called from the front to disperse them.

The Provisional government was split over the issue of discipline for mutinous troops. Dissension rent the soviets as well: Lenin's Bolsheviks were struggling to snatch control of these councils from the far more numerous and more moderate Mensheviks and Socialist Revolutionaries.

National elections were set for November 25. If Kerensky and his government could hold out until then they might win. Lenin knew it. So he did not wait for elections to decide whether the people approved of "All power to the soviets." On the night of November 7, troops and armed factory workers led by Lenin's Bolsheviks seized some of the principal government buildings and arrested government ministers. The Bolshevik-controlled battleship *Aurora* shelled the Winter Palace, which was Kerensky's headquarters, and the Admiralty. Kerensky attempted in vain to rally Cossacks outside the city. A battalion of women and a few military cadets resisted the *coup*, but they were quickly crushed. In important cities all over the country the Bolsheviks struck in the same way. In Moscow three thousand military cadets held out in the Kremlin for a week before they were beaten and their commander murdered and mutilated. But by that time Lenin was president of the Council of People's Commissars, which had taken over from the government, Leon Trotsky was commissar for foreign affairs, and Joseph Stalin was commissar of nationalities. Russia had a new autocracy.

A crowd of Bolsheviks set fire to zarist emblems; when the flames died down, the revolution had ended.

IX

RUSSIA SINCE THE CZARS

Soon after Lenin's *coup*, it became clear that bolshevism (or, as it soon came to be called, communism) was unacceptable to millions of Russians. The new regime termed itself a dictatorship of the working class. It was in reality a dictatorship of the small Communist party headed by Lenin and Trotsky. It was not the kind of government that intelligent Russians had been yearning for since the Decembrists' revolt more than ninety years before. Thousands fled the country. Many thousands more took up arms and remained to fight. A bloody civil war broke out in 1918 and raged for two years. Often it came close to sweeping away communism. But the opponents of the regime were split by dissension and they lacked the resources for a long war. The Communists, under the brilliant military leadership of Trotsky, triumphed.

Communism's triumph gave Russia a government which for much of the half century in which it has held power has borne a striking resemblance to that of the czars at their worst.

Because rebellion had been crushed but silent opposition had not, the Communists established a secret police system which differed from the czars' only in that it was more cruel and more efficient. Once again newspapers and books were strictly censored. Once again foreign ideas became suspect and people could not travel abroad. Once again exile to Siberia became the penalty for expressing thoughts disrespectful of the regime. Once again the many minorities who make up half of the population of the Soviet Union were cruelly persecuted.

In nothing is the resemblance between the czarist and Communist regimes stronger than in the character and methods of Joseph Stalin, who ruled Russia from 1928 to 1953. Stalin, who had become a bank robber early in the century to finance his revolutionary activities, had long been a minor figure in the Communist party and in its violent predecessors. He had risen at length to be party

general-secretary, a technical rather than a policy-making position. It seemed unlikely that he would go higher, for if Lenin died, Trotsky was next in line, and both of them distrusted and disliked Stalin.

But Stalin maneuvered quietly with all the skill and deviousness of Peter the Great's half-sister, Sophia. By the time Lenin died (1924) and his body was resting in its marble mausoleum outside the Kremlin wall in Red Square, Stalin was well on the way to establishing himself as dictator. Trotsky was soon in exile and some years later died at the hand of an assassin in Stalin's pay.

If Stalin resembled Sophia in political skill, he resembled Ivan the Terrible in his methods, which manifested themselves at their worst in his dealings with the peasants. By those dealings, Stalin showed that communism had not changed the basic relationship between Russia's rulers and its people. The conflict between Stalin and the peasants centered on Stalin's insistence that the peasants surrender their individual property rights and merge their farms into collectives.

Stalin pressed for the collectives because he believed that communism could not survive in Russia and could not be imposed on the rest of the world, as the Communists intended, unless Russia rapidly industrialized to produce the raw materials of warfare, primarily steel and fuels. He knew that he could get workers for new industries only from the farms. But the farms would have to be made more

Joseph Stalin was the Communists' all-powerful leader before World War II. After helping to win that war, he (in a marshal's uniform above) conferred with Roosevelt and Churchill at Yalta, the former winter resort of Russia's czars. There he tried to win the peace.

147

efficient by mechanization so that they could be worked with fewer hands when the peasants quit them for the factories.

With their age-old love of the land, the peasants resisted collectivization. Particularly stubborn were the peasants called kulaks, who had prospered as independent farmers since the reforms under the later czars. Stalin then ruthlessly ordered the liquidation of the kulaks as a class. He sent machine-gun squads to mow down thousands of defenseless people. He shipped whole villages off to Siberian and Arctic labor camps where their inhabitants lived under a new, more dreadful serfdom. The survivors reluctantly entered the collectives. But first they slaughtered their horses and cattle rather than turn them over to the government; then they worked as slowly as they dared. In the man-made famine that followed, millions of peasants died of hunger. There were more than 5,500,000 kulaks in 1928, shortly before Stalin's order went into effect; in 1934, only 149,000 remained. And by the beginning of World War II, when nearly all farms had been collectivized, a total of 10,000,000 lives had been sacrificed to satisfy Stalin's insistence on over-rapid industrialization of the country. The period of the first Five Year Plan, under which the industrialization was undertaken and which spanned the years 1928–32, was one of the most desperately inhuman in all Russian history.

Stalin did not hesitate to extend his ruthlessness beyond Russia's borders. Like the czars, he strove to expand the power, if not the boundaries, of the Russian empire. In the economically depressed Western world of the nineteen-thirties, Communist agents worked secretly in attempts to organize revolutions. When a fascist rebellion erupted into civil war in Spain in 1936, Stalin sent aid to the government of the Spanish Republic, then betrayed and virtually took over that government. In World War II, when the Germans met fierce defiance in Warsaw's ghetto, Stalin had a huge army just a little distance away, but he refused to help his beleaguered Polish allies because they were not Communists and because the Poles have always been traditional enemies of the Russians. Immediately after World War II, by internal subversion and external military pressure, he incorporated the nations of the Balkans into the Russian empire.

There is of course a vast difference between the Russian people and their rulers, as typified by Stalin. It is almost half a century that they have lived under communism. Three quarters of them have been born since 1917. Most have never known anything but a Communist dictatorship. They have read no newspapers except those controlled by their government, they have read no books not approved by the government. Few can travel abroad. Yet the desire for freedom persists among them. Russian young people quietly discuss forbidden Western ideas. Russian writers risk imprisonment to smuggle out to the West articles and books critical of Communist dictatorship. Despite the Communist scorn of religion, millions still go to church. Peasants still mock the system under which they live by producing more food in their little garden plots than on the great expanses of the collective farms.

They are not, however, stirring up revolution, and it is unlikely that another Russian revolution will explode to abolish communism. But, since Stalin's death in 1953, minor though encouraging changes have taken place in Russia. The power of the secret police has waned, and there is a new emphasis on a better life for the individual Russian, even at the expense of heavy industry.

Whether Russia will change course abruptly again, as it did so often under the czars, is unpredictable. But as communism's tragic beginnings in the October Revolution of 1917 become less immediate, the easier it is to see that what the Communists have done and are trying to do has been tried by Russians before. And although there is little reassurance to be found in Russian history, from the turbulent days of the Scythians up until today, there is a pattern of behavior that can be studied with profit for tomorrow.

UPI

The West got a penetrating look at Nikita Khrushchev in 1960 when he appeared at the U.N. Waving his arms and banging his shoe, he was as boisterous as Peter the Great.

149

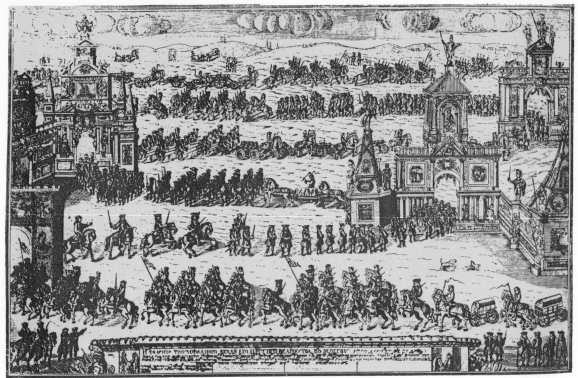

The army of Russia's Peter the Great marches triumphantly into Moscow after defeating the Swedish forces at Poltava in 1709. The battle did not end the war between the two countries, but broke the power and the spirit of Sweden's Charles XII.

AMERICAN HERITAGE
PUBLISHING CO., INC.

BOOK DIVISION
RICHARD M. KETCHUM, *Editor*

HORIZON CARAVEL BOOKS
RUSSELL BOURNE, *Editor*

MERVYN D. KAUFMAN, *Assistant Editor*

JUDITH HARKISON, *Chief Picture Researcher*

LUCY DAVIDSON, *Picture Researcher*

EVELYN H. REGISTER, *Picture Researcher*

ELAINE K. ANDREWS, *Copy Editor*

JANET CZARNETZKI, *Art Director*

GERTRUDIS FELIU, *European Bureau*

ACKNOWLEDGMENTS

The Editors are deeply indebted to the staff members of many private and public collections in which paintings, photographs, illuminated manuscripts, and articles of special importance to this book were found. Foremost among these collections are the Reference Library, The Metropolitan Museum of Art, New York City; the Slavonic Division, New York Public Library; the Prints and Photographic Division, Library of Congress; The Frick Art Reference Library, New York City; and The Free Library of Philadelphia. Special thanks are also owed to Alexander Kerensky, former President of Russia's Provisional government, and to Professor Henry L. Roberts, Director of Columbia University's Russian Institute, both of whom gave generously of their time and advice. In addition, the Editors wish to thank the following individuals and organizations for their assistance and for making available material in their collections:

Wilson Duprey, Prints Division, New York Public Library

A. Paramonov, State Tretyakov Gallery, Moscow

Messrs. Peter and Paul Schaffer, A La Vieille Russie, New York City

M. M. Ouspensky, State Historical Museum, Moscow

Special research and photography: Moscow—Audrey R. Topping; New York—Geoffrey Clements, Frank Lerner, Arnold Eagle, Karl Zimmer; London—Maureen Green; Italy—Maria Todorow, Ann Natanson; Tokyo— Arthur Miyazawa.

FURTHER REFERENCE

Readers interested in further exploring Russian art and memorabilia will find collections which they can visit in many American cities. An exhibition of Russian icons can be seen at the University of Oregon Museum of Art in Eugene. Russian glass is displayed in the Corning Museum of Glass, Corning, N.Y. Examples of Russia's cultural heritage are contained in the Museum of Russian Culture in San Francisco. Religious objects from the Russian Church can be seen at the Sheldon Jackson Junior College Museum, Sitka, Alaska, and at the Hammond Museum, Gloucester, Mass. Russian objects are on display at The Walters Art Gallery, Baltimore, Md.; the Virginia Museum of Fine Arts, Richmond; and the Los Angeles County Museum. Examples of Byzantine art can be found at The Dumbarton Oaks Research Library and Collection, Washington, D.C.; The Denver Art Museum; The Museum of Fine Arts of Houston; The Cleveland Museum of Art; and The Metropolitan Museum of Art, New York City.

For those who wish to read more about the history of Russia, the following books are recommended:

Carmichael, Joel. *An Illustrated History of Russia.* New York: Reynal & Company.

Charques, R. D. *A Short History of Russia.* New York: E. P. Dutton, 1961.

Clarkson, Jesse D. *A History of Russia.* New York: Random House, 1961.

De Caulaincourt, General Armand. *With Napoleon in Russia.* New York: Grosset & Dunlap Universal Library.

Duncan, David Douglas. *The Kremlin.* Greenwich, Conn.: Graphic, 1960.

Grey, Ian. *Peter the Great.* New York: J. B. Lippincott, 1960.

Gunther, John. *Inside Russia Today.* New York: Harper, 1958.

Hamilton, George Heard. *The Art and Architecture of Russia.* Baltimore: Penguin, 1954.

Kalb, Marvin. *Eastern Exposure.* New York: Farrar, Straus, 1958.

Kennan, George F. *Russia and the West Under Lenin and Stalin.* Boston: Little, Brown, 1961.

Lamb, Harold. *Genghis Khan.* New York: Garden City Publishing Co., 1927.

Lamb, Harold. *The March of Muscovy.* New York: Doubleday, 1948.

Maroger, Dominique. *The Memoirs of Catherine the Great.* New York: Macmillan.

Martin, John Stuart. *A Picture History of Russia.* New York: Crown, 1945.

Miller, Wright. *Russians as People.* New York: E. P. Dutton, 1961.

Mosse, W. E. *Alexander II and the Modernization of Russia.* New York: Macmillan, 1958.

Overstreet, Harry A. and Bonaro. *What We Must Know About Communism.* New York: Norton, 1958.

Pares, Bernard. *A History of Russia.* New York: Alfred A. Knopf, 1960.

Payne, Robert. *The Terrorists.* Funk & Wagnalls, New York: 1957.

Plievier, Theodor. *Stalingrad.* New York: Berkley Publishing Corp., 1948.

Rama Rau, Santha. *My Russian Journey.* New York: Harper, 1959.

Rice, Tamara Talbot. *The Scythians.* New York: Frederick A. Praeger, 1957.

Salisbury, Harrison E. *To Moscow and Beyond.* New York: Harper, 1960.

Savage, Katherine. *People and Power.* New York: Henry Z. Walck, Inc.

Tolstoy, Leo. *War and Peace.* New York: Random House.

Vernadsky, George. *A History of Russia.* New Haven: Yale University Press, 1954.

INDEX

Bold face indicates pages on which maps or illustrations appear

153

ST. ELIAS CHURCH
MUNHALL, PENNSYLVANIA